BAY AREA GOL YO-EKS-530

for 1991

INCLUDES THE ORIGINAL COUNTIES OF:

ALAMEDA
CONTRA COSTA
MARIN
MONTEREY
NAPA
SAN BENITO
SAN FRANCISCO
SAN MATEO
SANTA CLARA
SANTA CRUZ
SOLANO
SONOMA

PLUS COVERAGE IN:

SACRAMENTO
SAN JOAQUIN

By:

Locations Plus...

All information contained in this publication was provided or derived from provided material
by the individual golf courses. Every attempt was made to verify all information at the time of
printing and is believed, by the publishers, to be both accurate and complete. However, due to
the rapidness of change, not all information can be guaranteed to be error free. If you believe
that an error or an omission exists, please contact the publishers at the following address.

LOCATIONS PLUS...
3431 Hilary Drive
San Jose, CA 95124
(408) 371-0600

CONTENTS

CONTENTS

CONTENTS

CONTENTS

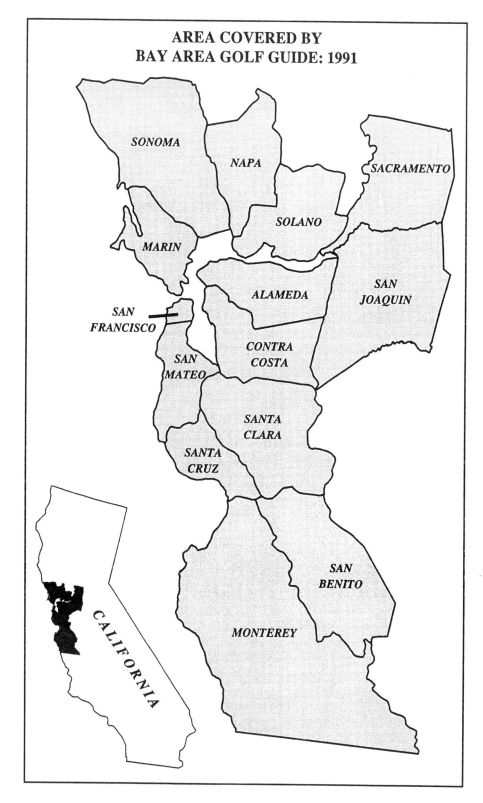

AREA COVERED BY
BAY AREA GOLF GUIDE: 1991

SONOMA

NAPA

SACRAMENTO

SOLANO

MARIN

SAN
FRANCISCO

ALAMEDA

SAN
JOAQUIN

SAN
MATEO

CONTRA
COSTA

SANTA
CLARA

SANTA
CRUZ

SAN
BENITO

MONTEREY

CALIFORNIA

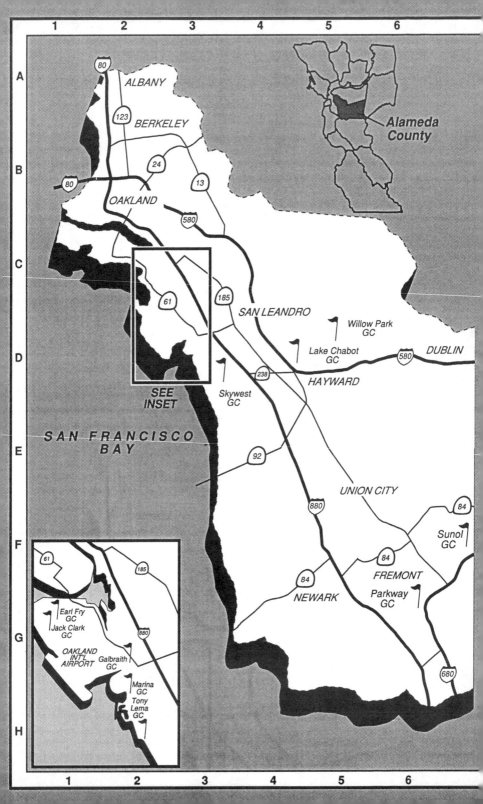

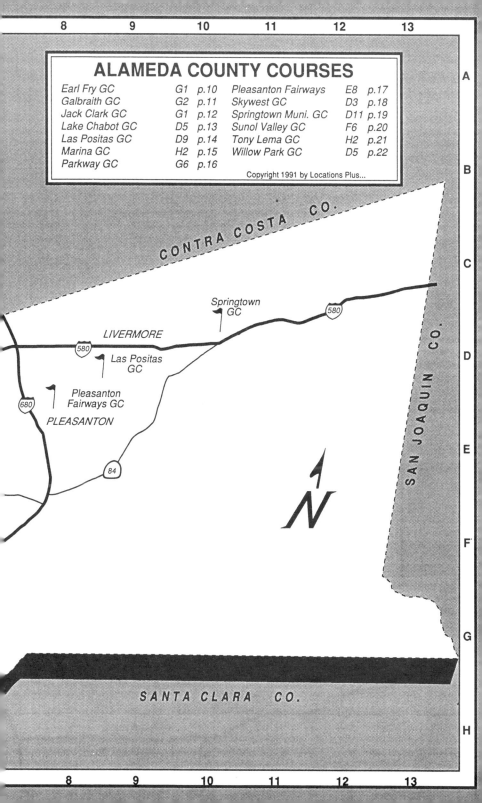

ALAMEDA COUNTY COURSES

Earl Fry GC	G1	p.10	Pleasanton Fairways	E8	p.17
Galbraith GC	G2	p.11	Skywest GC	D3	p.18
Jack Clark GC	G1	p.12	Springtown Muni. GC	D11	p.19
Lake Chabot GC	D5	p.13	Sunol Valley GC	F6	p.20
Las Positas GC	D9	p.14	Tony Lema GC	H2	p.21
Marina GC	H2	p.15	Willow Park GC	D5	p.22
Parkway GC	G6	p.16			

Earl Fry Golf Course

1 Clubhouse Memorial Road
Alameda, CA 94501

(415) 522-4321

18 Hole Course

1991 Green Fees:

	Weekdays	Weekends
9 Holes:	$6.00	$8.00
18 Holes:	$10.00	$13.00

Twilight Rate: $8.00
Senior Discount: $7.00 weekdays only

Equipment Rental:

Golf Cars - 9 Holes: $10.00   Golf Cars - 18 Holes: $16.00
        Pull Carts: $2.00   Clubs: $10.00

Amenities:

Club Pro: Steve Videtta   Lessons: $25 / 30 Minutes
A Practice Putting Green and a Driving Range are available. Bucket prices: $1.50 - $4.50. The Alameda Restaurant is open from 6 a.m. until 8 p.m. for your convenience. A cocktail lounge is also available. Check at the Pro Shop for details on their Early Bird cart rentals. Reservations can be made seven days in advance. They are busiest Wednesdays thru Sundays, least busy on Mondays.

Course Highlights:

Alameda Golf Complex consists of 2, 18 hole courses, Earl Fry and Jack Clark. Earl Fry was the first to open in 1927. The course ratings from the Men's Tees are: Championship 68.0, Regular 66.6. Course ratings from the Women's Tees are: White 72.1, Red 70.2. Par for the course is 71. Yardages range from 6,141 to 5,505. This is a very challenging course with an abundance of water hazards.

Galbraith Golf Course

10505 Doolittle Drive
Oakland, CA 94603

(415) 569-9411

OAKLAND INTERNATIONAL AIRPORT

Lew Galbraith Golf Course

18 Hole Course

1991 Green Fees:

	Weekdays	Weekends
9 Holes:	n.a.	n.a.
18 Holes:	$11.00	$15.00
Twilight Rate: After 1 p.m.	$6.00	$9.00

Senior Discount: $8.00 on weekdays only.

Equipment Rental:

Golf Cars - 9 Holes: Golf Cars - 18 Holes: $15.00
Pull Carts: $2.50   Clubs: $10.00

Amenities:

Club Pro: Dan Osterberg   Lessons: $25 / 30 Minutes
Galbraith Golf Course offers a Practice Putting Green, Chipping
Green and a Driving Range. Bucket prices: $1.50 - $7.00. The
Snack Bar is open from 6 a.m. until 8 p.m. The Pro Shop will help
you in filling your immediate golfing needs. Reservations can be
made one week in advance beginning at 6:00 a.m. , Sat. for Sat. etc.

Course Highlights:

This 18 hole championship course opened in 1967. It is a long
course measuring 6,777 yards from the Blue Tees, 6,298 yards from
the White Tees and 5,732 yards from the Red Tees. Course ratings
are: 71.1, 69.9, and 71.7, respectively. Par for the course is 72. They
have just completed putting a water swell in front of the green on the
10th hole adding a bit of a challenge. Overall the course is flat and is
easy to walk. There is a sufficient amount of trees and foliage to
attract many varieties of wildlife. This course is sometimes referrred
to as being a refuge to some of the endangered species.

11

Jack Clark Golf Course

1 Clubhouse Memorial Rd.
Alameda, CA 94501

(415) 522-4321

18 Hole Course

1991 Green Fees:	Weekdays	Weekends
9 Holes:	$6.00	$8.00
18 Holes:	$10.00	$13.00

Twilight Rate: $8.00
Senior Discount: $8.00 weekdays only

Equipment Rental:
Golf Cars - 9 Holes: $10.00   Golf Cars - 18 Holes: $16.00
Pull Carts: $2.00   Clubs: $10.00

Amenities:
Club Pro: Steve Videtta   Lessons: $25 / 30 Minutes
A Practice Putting Green and a Driving Range are available. Bucket
prices: $1.50 - $4.50. The Alameda Restaurant is open from 6 a.m.
until 8 p.m. for your convenience. A cocktail lounge is also available. Check at the Pro Shop for details on their Early Bird cart
rentals. Reservations can be made seven days in advance.

Course Highlights:
Jack Clark was added to the Alameda Golf Complex in 1956. This
18 hole course is rated 69.4 from the Championship Tees, and 67.3
from the Regular Tees. Course ratings from the Women's Tees are:
White 73.0, Red 69.3. Par for the course is 71. Yardage for the
course range from 6,559 to 5,473. This is the longest of the two
courses, but not by much. If your golf shots often head in the
direction of water hazards you would be better off playing this
course, it runs a little dryer than the Earl Fry course.

12

Lake Chabot Municipal Golf Course

End of Golf Links Rd.
Oakland, CA 94605

(415) 351-5812

18 Hole Course

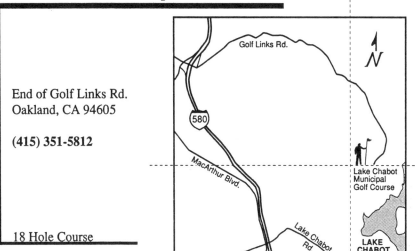

1991 Green Fees:

	Weekdays	Weekends
9 Holes:	n.a.	n.a.
18 Holes:	$10.00	$14.00
Twilight Rate: After 1 or 3 p.m.	$6.00	$9.00

Senior Discount: $16.00 Monthly Ticket + Surcharge

Equipment Rental:

Golf Cars - 9 Holes:	Golf Cars - 18 Holes:	$15.00
Pull Carts: n.a.	Clubs:	$12.00

Amenities:

Club Pro: Jeffrey Dennis   Lessons: $30 / Lesson
Lake Chabot Golf Course has a Practice Putting Green and a Driving
Range. Bucket prices: $1.50 - $3.50. Their Coffee Shop is open
from dawn to dusk. The Pro Shop handles a complete line of golf
equipment. Weekend reservations are taken on the prior Monday
beginning at 6:00 a.m. and for weekdays, seven days in advance.

Course Highlights:

Lake Chabot Golf Course has been in operation since 1923. It is one
of the few courses that has a par 6 hole. It is 668 yards long and is
the last hole on the course. Total yardage from the Men's Tees
is 6,011 and 5,278 from the Women's Tees. The course is rated 67.4,
and 68.8, respectively. Par is 70/71. There is one par 6 hole, three
par 5 holes, five par 3 holes, leaving the remaining 9 holes with a par
of 4. This course hosts the Lake Chabot Pro-Am and the Oakland
City Tournaments in September, and the Charles Peoples Pro-Am in
May.

13

Las Positas Golf Course

Clubhouse Drive
Livermore, CA 94551

(415) 443-3122

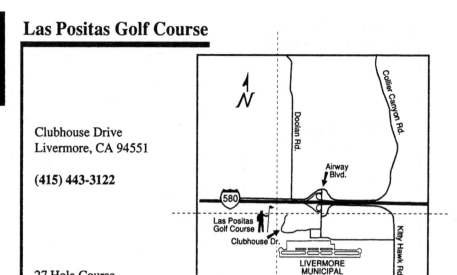

27 Hole Course

1991 Green Fees:	Weekdays	Weekends
9 Holes:	$10.00*	$13.00*
18 Holes:	$14.00*	$22.00*
Twilight Rate:	$10.00	$13.00
Senior Discount:	Mondays only	

Equipment Rental:

Golf Cars - 9 Holes: Golf Cars - 18 Holes: $18.00
Pull Carts: $2.00   Clubs: $2.00

Amenities:

Club Pro: Dan Lippstreu   Lessons: $25 / 30 Minutes
Las Positas offers a Practice Putting Green, Chipping Green and a
Driving Range. Bucket prices: $2.00 - $4.00. A Clubhouse and
lounge are available. The Pro Shop will help fill your immediate
golfing needs. Weekend reservations can be made on the prior
Tuesday beginning at 7:00 a.m., for weekdays, one week in advance.
Their busiest day of the week is Saturday, least busy day is Tuesday.

Course Highlights:

*The Green Fees listed above are for the 18 hole course. For the
executive 9 hole course, Green Fees are: $9.00 on Weekdays, and
$11.00 on Weekends. This course has undergone a complete
overhaul which was completed in July of 1990. The course has been
expanded to include 27 holes. Par for the 18 hole course is 72 and
the 9 hole executive course has a par of 31.

14

Marina Golf Course

13800 Neptune Drive
San Leandro, CA 94577

(415) 895-2164

9 Hole Course

1991 Green Fees:

	Weekdays	Weekends
9 Holes:	$4.00	$5.00
18 Holes:	$6.00	$8.00

Twilight Rate:
Senior Discount: Residents of San Leandro only.

Equipment Rental:

Golf Cars - 9 Holes:	$6.00	Golf Cars - 18 Holes:	$12.00
Pull Carts:	$3.00	Clubs:	$10.00

Amenities:

Club Pro: Steve Elbe   Lessons: $25 / 30 Minutes
This course is the 9 hole Executive course of the San Leandro Golf
Complex. They have a Practice Putting Green and lighted Driving
Range. Bucket prices: $1.25 - $4.00. The Brass Putter Restaurant is
open from dawn until 8 p.m. The Steve Elbe Golf Shop carries a
complete line of golf merchandise. Reservations can be made one
week in advance beginning at 6:00 a.m.

Course Highlights:

This course opened originally with 9 holes in 1963. A temporary
additional 9 was added in 1974 pending completion of the Tony
Lema Golf Course, a championship 18 hole course. Marina reverted
back to its' original layout and is a nine hole course today. With only
1,658 yards, par 29, distance is not a major factor when playing this
course, but accuracy is. Only two of the holes are par 4's and the rest
are par 3's. You might consider this a warm-up course before
starting out on Tony Lema's.

15

Parkway Golf Course

3400 Stevenson Blvd.
Fremont, CA 94538

(415) 656-6862

9 Hole Course

1991 Green Fees:

	Weekdays	Weekends
9 Holes:	$5.50	n.a.
18 Holes:	$7.50	$11.00

Twilight Rate: n.a.
Senior Discount: $4.50 / 9 holes, $6.50 18 holes, applies weekdays.

Equipment Rental:

Golf Cars - 9 Holes:	n.a.	Golf Cars - 18 Holes:	n.a.
Pull Carts:	$2.00	Clubs:	$4.00

Amenities:

Club Pro: Mike Pope   Lessons: $20 / 30 Minutes
Parkway Golf Course offers a Practice Putting Green and a Driving Cage. They have a Snack Bar and lounge for your convenience. A Pro Shop will help in filling your immediate golfing needs. Reservations can be made one week in advance beginning at 7:00 a.m. Their busiest day of the week is Sunday, least busy day is Monday.

Course Highlights:

Parkway Golf Course originally opened in 1971 with 18 holes. It has recently lost it's back 9 holes and is now a 9 hole, par 3 course. It is a true delight for the golfer who prefers to play nine holes. Just because this is a par 3, don't assume it is an easy course. You will find plenty of sandtraps and water hazards to challenge your accuracy. Total yardage of the course is now 1,024. It is rated 49.9 for the Men and 52.1 for the Women. Slope rating: 67. Parkway hosts the Saturday Men's Championship, the Anniversary Tournament and Club Tournaments each year.

Pleasanton Fairways Golf Course

4501 Pleasanton Ave.
Pleasanton, CA 94566

(415) 462-4653

9 Hole Course

1991 Green Fees:

	Weekdays	Weekends
9 Holes:	$6.00	$7.00
18 Holes:	$11.50	$13.50

Twilight Rate: n.a.
Senior Discount: $5.25 Wkdays. / $6.50 Wknds. for 9 Holes

Equipment Rental:

Golf Cars - 9 Holes: n.a.	Golf Cars - 18 Holes: n.a.
Pull Carts: $1.50	Clubs: $6.00

Amenities:

Club Pro: Bill Corbett   Lessons:
Pleasanton Fairways offers a Practice Putting Green, Chipping Green and a Driving Range. Bucket prices: $1.75 - $3.50. Only irons are allowed on this range. They have a newer regulation driving range across the road. The Snack Bar is open daily for your convenience, serving a variety of refreshments. The Pro Shop is complete. Reservations are taken Monday thru Sunday.

Course Highlights:

Construction on this nine hole course was completed in 1974. To add country charm, it is situated in the center of the oval race track in the Alameda Country Fairgrounds. As you might guess, it is a fairly short course measuring 1,755 yards. Par for the course is 29 and the course record is 25 which indicates it is not an easy course. There are three par 4 holes, and the rest are par 3's. Course rating is 54.4.

Skywest Golf Course

1401 Golf Course Road
Hayward, CA 94541

(415) 278-6188

18 Hole Course

1991 Green Fees:

	Weekdays	Weekends
9 Holes:	$7.00	*
18 Holes:	$11.00	$13.00

Twilight Rate: *$8.50 - 9 holes after 3 p.m. on weekends
Senior Discount: Monthly tickets for residents only

Equipment Rental:

Golf Cars - 9 Holes: $8 / $9   Golf Cars - 18 Holes: $13 / $14
  Pull Carts: $2.50   Clubs: n.a.

Amenities:

Club Pro: Cheryl Pastore   Lessons: $25 / 30 Minutes
A Practice Putting Green and a Driving Range are available at
Skywest Golf Course. Bucket prices: $2.50 - $3.50. The Skywest
Restaurant is open daily from sunrise to sunset. The Pro Shop carries
a complete line of golf accessories. Reservations can be made seven
days in advance, Sat. for Sat., etc. beginning at 6:00 a.m. Their
busiest day is Friday, least busy on Thursday.

Course Highlights:

This 18 hole course opened in 1965. Major renovations have just
been completed, such as installation of an automatic sprinkling
system and new cart paths. From the Championship Tees it is 6,930
yards long, rated 72.8 / 121. From the Men's White Tees it is 6,540
yards long, rated 70.9 / 116. Women's yardage is 6,171, rated 74.3 /
123.   Par for the course is 72 for the Men and 73 for the Women.
Course records are 65 from both sets of Men's Tees and a 68 from the
Ladies' Tees. Skywest regularly hosts the Hayward City Championship Tournament during February.

Springtown Municipal Golf Course

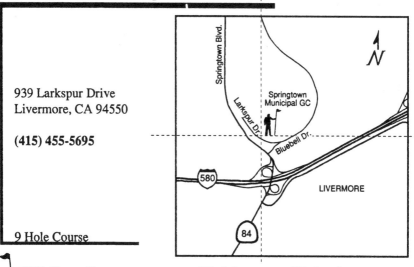

939 Larkspur Drive
Livermore, CA 94550

(415) 455-5695

9 Hole Course

1991 Green Fees:

	Weekdays	Weekends
9 Holes:	$9.00	$10.00
18 Holes:	$11.00	$14.00

Twilight Rate: n.a.
Senior Discount: Monthly pass: $50 single, $65 married couple.

Equipment Rental:

Golf Cars - 9 Holes: Golf Cars - 18 Holes: $18.00
    Pull Carts: $2.00   Clubs: $5.00

Amenities:

Club Pro: Keith Boam   Lessons: $20 / 45 Minutes
Springtown Municipal offers a Practice Putting Green, Chipping area
and a Driving Cage. The price of a bucket of balls is $2.00. The
Springtown Coffee Shop serves full breakfast and lunch, and an
assortment of beverages, including beer and wine. Their Pro Shop
carries a complete line of golf accessories. Reservations can be made
at any time. Their least busy day of the week is Tuesday.

Course Highlights:

This 9 hole course opened approximately 28 years ago. It has a
separate set of tees for playing a second nine. The course measures
5,710 yards long from the Men's Tees and 5,332 yards from the
Women's Tees. Par for the course is 70. The course is rated 65.4
from the Men's White and Blue Tees, and 69.5 from the Women's
Red and White Tees. The course is well varied with doglegs, water
hazards and sandtraps. The fairways are open but you still have the
possibility of hitting a tree now and then.

19

Sunol Valley Golf Course

6900 Mission Road
Sunol, CA 94586

(415) 862-2404

Two 18 Hole Courses

1991 Green Fees:

	Weekdays	Weekends
9 Holes:	n.a.	n.a.
18 Holes:	$18.00	$40.00*
Twilight Rate: After 2:00	$14.00	$15.00
Senior Discount: Monthly purchase		

Equipment Rental: *Golf Car included in weekend Green Fees

Golf Cars - 9 Holes: n.a.	Golf Cars - 18 Holes: $24.00
Pull Carts: n.a.	Clubs: $20.00

Amenities:

Club Pro: Jerry Thormann   Lessons: $25 / Lesson
Sunol Valley has two 18 hole golf courses, The Palms and The
Cypress. They have a Practice Putting Green and Chipping
Green, but no Driving Range. Their cafe is open from 6 a.m.
until 5 p.m., a cocktail lounge is also available. A Golf Car is
mandatory on weekends. Reservations can be made seven days
in advance beginning at 6:30 a.m., Sat. for Sat., etc.

Course Highlights:

The Sunol Valley Golf Courses are set in the scenic valley of
Mission Hills. The Palms Course is the longest of the two courses.
From the Blue Tees it is 6,843 yards long, from the White Tees it is
6,409 yards long and from the Red Tees it is 5,997 yards long. This
is the wider of the two courses. Cypress Course, being shorter, is
6,195 yards from the Blue Tees, 5,801 yards from the White Tees,
and 5,458 yards long from the Women's Tees. This course will
require a little more straight shooting on the part of the golfer
because of the narrow fairways. Par for both of the courses is 72.

Tony Lema Golf Course

13800 Neptune Drive
San Leandro, CA 94577

(415) 895-2162

18 Hole Course

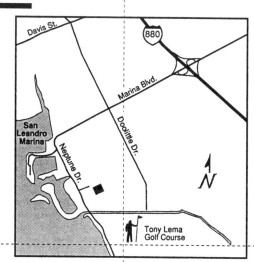

1991 Green Fees:

	Weekdays	Weekends
9 Holes:	n.a.	n.a.
18 Holes:	$9.50	$13.50
Twilight Rate: 2:00 p.m.	$6.50	$9.50

Senior Discount: San Leandro residents-weekdays only

Equipment Rental:

Golf Cars - 9 Holes:	Golf Cars - 18 Holes: $16.00
Pull Carts: $3.00	Clubs: $10.00

Amenities:

Club Pro: Steve Elbe   Lessons: $25 / 30 Minutes
This 18 hole course is part of the San Leandro Golf Complex.
Available here is a Practice Putting Green and lighted Driving
Range. Bucket prices: $1.50 - $4.50. The Brass Putter Restaurant is
open from dawn until 8 p.m., a cocktail lounge is also available. The
Steve Elbe Golf Shop carries a complete line of golf merchandise.
Reservations can be made one week in advance starting at 6:00 a.m.

Course Highlights:

This championship 18 hole course was completed in 1983. It is
sitting on the eastern edge of San Francisco Bay, across from the
yacht harbor, and an assortment of fine restaurants. Total yardage
from the Championship Tees is 6,636, rating is 69.2; yardage from
the Regular Tees is 6,175, rating is 67.1. Women's total yardage is
5,718, rating is 71.3, slope is 108. Par for the course is 72.
Tony Lema Golf Course regularly hosts the Coor's sponsored
People's Pro-Am Tournament.

Willow Park Golf Course

17007 Redwood Road
Castro Valley, CA 94546

(415) 537-8989

18 Hole Course

1991 Green Fees:

	Weekdays	Weekends
9 Holes:	$8.00	$10.00
18 Holes:	$12.00	$16.00

Twilight Rate: n.a.
Senior Discount: n.a.

Equipment Rental:

Golf Cars - 9 Holes:	Golf Cars - 18 Holes: $16.00
Pull Carts: $2.00	Clubs: n.a.

Amenities:

Club Pro: Bob Bruce   Lessons: $16 / 30 Minutes
Willow Park Golf Course offers a Practice Putting Green and a
Driving Range. Bucket prices: $1.00 - $2.00. Their restaurant is
open from 10 a.m. until 10 p.m. every day except Mondays. A
cocktail lounge is also available. A complete line of golf accessories
can be found at the Pro Shop. Weekend reservations can be made on
the Monday prior in early a.m., for weekdays ten days in advance.

Course Highlights:

This Par 71, eighteen hole golf course opened in January of 1967.
The course record of 63 has not been beaten since 1968. Yardage
from the Championship Tees is 6,227, from the Men's regular Tees it
is 5,465 and it is 5,200 from the Women's Tees. There is a lovely
creek making its way through this course which, as you might guess,
often comes into play. There is enough variation in the landscape at
Willow Park to keep most golfers interested.

22

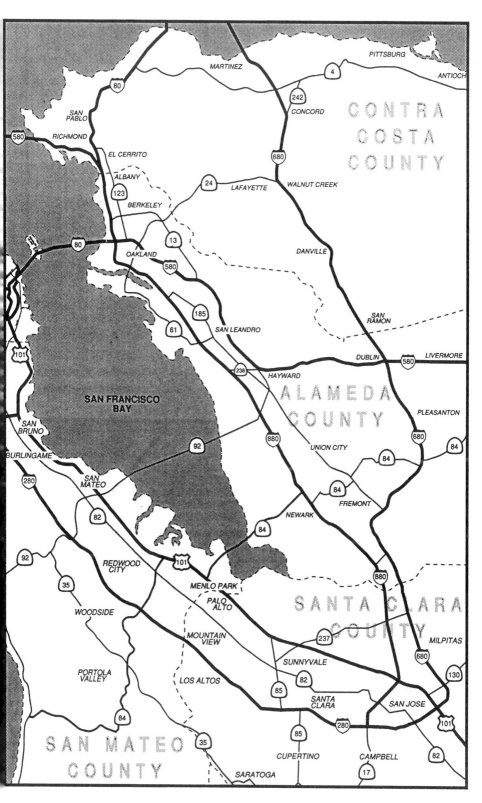

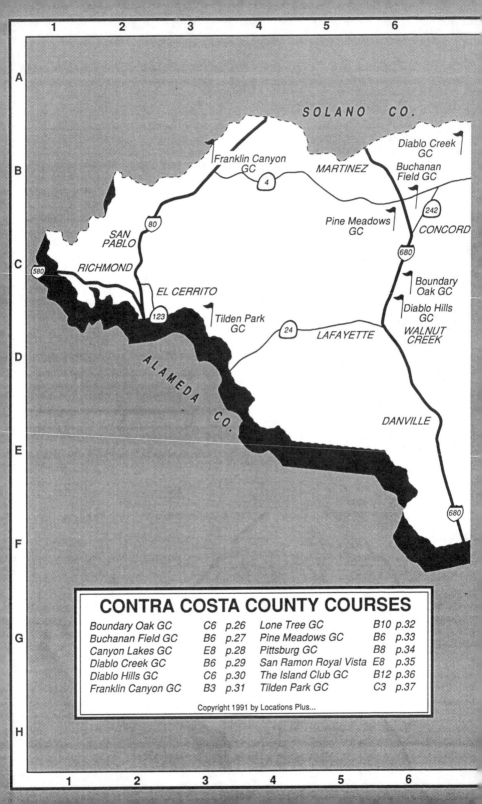

	1	2	3	4	5	6

SOLANO CO.

Diablo Creek GC

MARTINEZ

Buchanan Field GC

Franklin Canyon GC

4

242

Pine Meadows GC

CONCORD

80

SAN PABLO

680

RICHMOND

580

Boundary Oak GC

EL CERRITO

Diablo Hills GC

123

Tilden Park GC

24

LAFAYETTE

WALNUT CREEK

ALAMEDA CO.

DANVILLE

680

CONTRA COSTA COUNTY COURSES

Boundary Oak GC	C6	p.26	Lone Tree GC	B10	p.32
Buchanan Field GC	B6	p.27	Pine Meadows GC	B6	p.33
Canyon Lakes GC	E8	p.28	Pittsburg GC	B8	p.34
Diablo Creek GC	B6	p.29	San Ramon Royal Vista	E8	p.35
Diablo Hills GC	C6	p.30	The Island Club GC	B12	p.36
Franklin Canyon GC	B3	p.31	Tilden Park GC	C3	p.37

	1	2	3	4	5	6

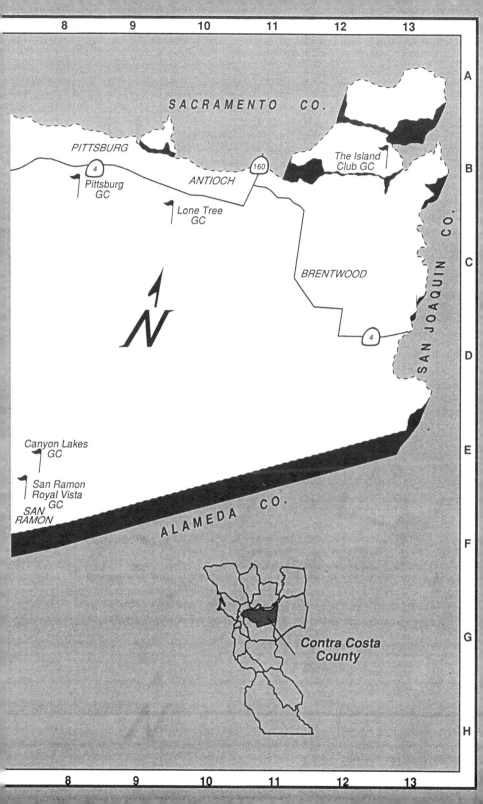

Boundary Oak Golf Course

3800 Valley Vista Road
Walnut Creek, CA 94598

(415) 934-6211

18 Hole Course

1991 Green Fees:

	Weekdays	Weekends
9 Holes:	$9.00	$12.00
18 Holes:	$13.00	$17.00

Twilight Rate: After 2:00 p.m. $7.00
Senior Discount: With weekly play cards.

Equipment Rental:

Golf Cars - 9 Holes: $12.00	Golf Cars - 18 Holes: $20.00
Pull Carts: $3.00	Clubs: $10.00

Amenities:

Club Pro: Robert T. Boldt   Lessons: 6 for $150
A Practice Putting Green, Chipping Green and a Driving Range are available. Bucket prices: $2.50 - $4.50. Their restaurant and lounge is open from dawn to dusk. Their Pro Shop is complete. Weekday reservations can be made by phone on Sundays starting at 9:00 a.m. and for weekends starting at 1:00 p.m. Walnut Creek residents receive a discount on Green Fees.

Course Highlights:

This 18 hole course opened in 1969. They regularly host the Contra Costa Amateur in mid July. From the Championship Tees the yardage is 6,788 and it is rated 72.0. From the Regular Tees it is 6,406 yards long and rated 70.2. The Women's yardage is 5,705, it is rated 72.1 - slope 117. Par for the course is 72. The course record is held by Craig Elliott with a 65 from the Championship Tees.

Buchanan Field Golf Course

3330 Concord Avenue
Concord, CA 94520

(415) 682-1846

9 Hole Course

1991 Green Fees:

	Weekdays	Weekends
9 Holes:	$7.50	$9.00
18 Holes:	$11.50	$14.00

Twilight Rate: n.a.
Senior Discount: $6.00 / 9 holes - $55 for 10 plays - weekdays only

Equipment Rental:

Golf Cars - 9 Holes: $9.00   Golf Cars - 18 Holes:
Pull Carts: $2.00   Clubs: $5.00

Amenities:

Club Pro: Tim Sullivan   Lessons: $25 / 30 Minutes
Buchanan Field Golf Course offers a Practice Putting Green and a
Driving Range. Bucket prices: $4.00 - $5.00. The Back-9 Restaurant is open from 7 a.m. until 5 p.m. for your convenience. The Pro Shop carries a full line of golf equipment. Reservations can be made one week in advance. Their busiest day is Saturday, least busy day is Monday.

Course Highlights:

This public nine hole course opened in 1961. Since then they have planted 400 trees to encourage more accuracy in the golfer's shots. This is a challenging nine holes, it plays for a total of 2,616 yards. Par for the Men is 33, Women's par is 36. The course rating for 18 holes is 63.0 for the Men, and 64.0 for the Women. The course is fairly flat and is ideal for the beginner golfer.

27

Canyon Lakes Country Club

640 Bollinger Canyon Way
San Ramon, CA 94583

(415) 867-0600

18 Hole Course

1991 Green Fees:

	Weekdays	Weekends
9 Holes:	$29.00	$32.00
18 Holes:	$50.00	$55.00

Twilight Rate: n.a.
Senior Discount: n.a.

Equipment Rental: Golf Cars included in Green Fees

Golf Cars - 9 Holes: Golf Cars - 18 Holes:
Pull Carts: n.a.   Clubs: $15.00

Amenities:

Club Pro: Russ Dicks   Lessons: $30 / 30 Minutes
Canyon Lakes is open every day except Mondays. A Practice
Putting Green is the only warm-up practice facility offered. Their
new clubhouse opened in early spring. Reservations can be made
seven days in advance. Their busiest days are Fridays thru Sundays,
least busy day is Tuesday. Use of a golf car is mandatory; it is
included in the Green Fee.

Course Highlights:

This 18 hole golf course, recently opened in 1987, is located in the
rolling hills of San Ramon. The course name, Canyon Lakes,
properly describes the scenic landscape. Yardage from the Championship Tees is 6,379 and from the Men's Tees it is 5,975. It is rated
70.1 and 68.2, respectively. From the Women's Tees it is 5,234
yards long and is rated 69.3. Par for the course is 71, the course
record stands at 65.

Diablo Creek Golf Course

4050 Port Chicago Highway
Concord, CA 94522

(415) 686-6262

18 Hole Course

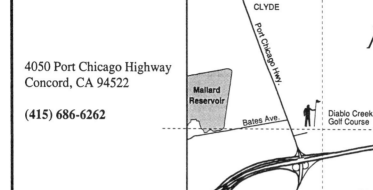

1991 Green Fees:

	Weekdays	Weekends
9 Holes:	*$8.00	*$11.00
18 Holes:	$14.00	$17.00

Twilight Rate: *After 2 / 4 p.m. or before 7:30 a.m.
Senior Discount:

Equipment Rental:

Golf Cars - 9 Holes: $9.00   Golf Cars - 18 Holes: $16.00
Pull Carts: $3.00   Clubs: $10.00

Amenities:

Club Pro: John Oderda   Lessons: $20 / 30 Minutes
Diablo Creek Golf Course offers a Practice Putting Green and a
Driving Range. Bucket prices: $2.00 - $3.75. Their full restaurant is
open daily from 6 a.m. until 10 p.m. Their Pro Shop is complete.
Reduced Green Fees available to Concord residents and they may
make weekend reservations on the prior Saturday. Non-residents
may reserve tee times on the prior Mondays.

Course Highlights:

Diablo Creek Golf Course originally opened as a 9 hole course in
1962. In 1972 an additional 9 holes were added. This beautiful 18
hole course at Diablo Creek has been rated as one of the Top Three
Public Courses for conditions in Northern California. Each year they
host the Concord City 2 Man Best Ball Tournament.

Diablo Hills Golf Course

1551 Marchbanks Drive
Walnut Creek, CA 94598

(415) 939-7372

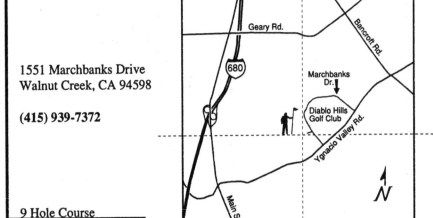

9 Hole Course

1991 Green Fees:

	Weekdays	Weekends
9 Holes:	$11.00	$15.00
18 Holes:	$18.00	$30.00

Twilight Rate: n.a.
Senior Discount: $9.00 / 9 Holes weekdays only; Jrs. $5.50

Equipment Rental:

Golf Cars - 9 Holes: $12.00	Golf Cars - 18 Holes: $24.00
Pull Carts: $2.00	Clubs: $5.00

Amenities:

Club Pro: Nick Andrakin   Lessons: $30 / 30 Minutes
Diablo Hills Golf Course offers a Practice Putting Green, Chipping
Green but no Driving Range. The Greenery Restaurant is open from
7 a.m. to 11 p.m. daily, a lounge is also available. Their Pro Shop
will help fill your immediate golfing needs. Weekend reservations
can be made anytime and they take weekday reservations one month
in advance. Their busiest day is Sunday, least busy on Thursdays.

Course Highlights:

This 9 hole course opened in 1975. It winds its way through a
picturesque setting of condominiums. When playing this course you
need to bring your sandwedge for it is heavily sprinkled with
sandtraps, but you can leave your ball retriever at home because it
does not have any water hazards. Men's yardage from the Blue Tees
is 2,302, and from the Women's Red Tees it is 2,173. Par for the
course is 34. Diablo Hills regularly hosts the Singh's Invitational
Golf Tournament.

30

Franklin Canyon Golf Course

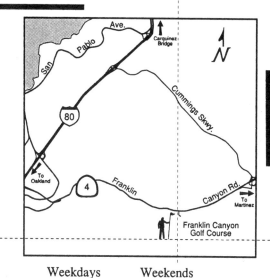

California Highway 4
Rodeo, CA 94572

(415) 799-6191

18 Hole Course

1991 Green Fees:

	Weekdays	Weekends
9 Holes:	n.a.	n.a.
18 Holes:	$16.00	$25.00
Twilight Rate:	$9.00	$13.00
Senior Discount: n.a.		

Equipment Rental:

Golf Cars - 9 Holes:	Golf Cars - 18 Holes: $20.00
Pull Carts: $3.00	Clubs: $15.00

Amenities:

Club Pro: Gill Flynn   Lessons: $32 / 60 Minutes
This golf course offers a Practice Putting Green, Chipping Green and a Driving Range. Bucket prices: $2.00 - $4.00. Their Snack Bar is open from dawn until 5 p.m. daily, a cocktail lounge is also available. The Pro Shop carries a complete line of golf accessories. Weekend reservations can be made seven days in advance beginning at 6:00 a.m. Busiest day is Saturday, least busy day is Tuesday.

Course Highlights:

This 18 hole course, designed by Robert Muir Graves, opened in March of 1968. The Clubhouse and Pro Shop were added in 1970. From the Championship Tees it plays for 6,776 yards and is rated 70.9. From the Regular Men's Tees it is 6,202 yards long and is rated 68.9. Yardage from the Women's Tees is 5,516 and is rated 71.2. Overall par for the course is 72. The course record stands at 63. Franklin Canyon annually hosts the Northern California Firefighters Open, the Northern CA Seniors Open and the West County Tournament. This is a fairly long and difficult course for any experienced level of golfer.

31

Lone Tree Golf Course

4800 Lone Tree Way
Antioch, CA 95431

(415) 757-5200

18 Hole Course

1991 Green Fees:

	Weekdays	Weekends
9 Holes:	$7.00	$10.00
18 Holes:	$8.50	$11.00

Twilight Rate: $7.00
Senior Discount: n.a.

Equipment Rental:

Golf Cars - 9 Holes: Golf Cars - 18 Holes: $14.00
    Pull Carts: $3.00   Clubs: $5.00

Amenities:

Club Pro: Pat Cain   Lessons: $20 / 30 Minutes
Lone Tree Golf Course offers a Practice Putting Green and a Driving
Range. Bucket prices: $1.00 - $2.00. Their Snack Bar is open from
dawn to dusk. A cocktail lounge is also available. The Pro Shop
carries a complete line of golf equipment. Weekend reservations can
be made on the Saturday prior, seven days in advance for weekdays.
Their busiest day is Saturday, least busy day is Monday.

Course Highlights:

Lone Tree is an eighteen hole, championship course. It falls in the
middle between difficult and easy. It is a pleasant course to play,
having a fair amount of hills and trees. From the Championship
Blue Tees the total yardage is 6,387, from the Regular White Tees
it is 6,073 and from the Women's Red Tees it is 5,769. Course
ratings are: 69.8, 67.8 and 71.8, respectively. Overall par for the
course is 72.

Pine Meadows Public Course

451 Vine Hill Way
Martinez, CA 94553

(415) 288-2881

9 Hole Course

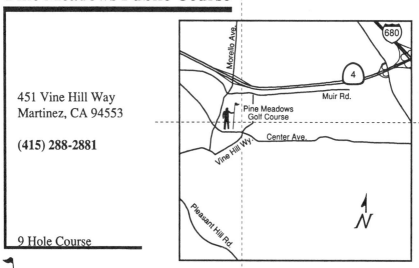

1991 Green Fees:

	Weekdays	Weekends
9 Holes:	$6.00	$8.00
18 Holes:	$10.00	$14.00
Twilight Rate: After 3:00 weekends only		$6.00
Senior Discount:	$5.00	$8.00

Equipment Rental:

Golf Cars - 9 Holes: $8.00   Golf Cars - 18 Holes: $16.00
          Pull Carts: $2.00   Clubs: $4.00

Amenities:

Club Pro: n.a.   Lessons:
A Practice Putting Green is available here at Pine Meadows, but no
Chipping Green or Driving Range. A Pro Shop will assist you in
completing your immediate golfing needs. A cocktail lounge is also
available. Reservations can be made at anytime.

Course Highlights:

Pine Meadows Golf Course opened in 1966. This 9 hole, par 3
course sits on approximately 32 acres of land located in residential
Martinez. It is a well maintained, straight, treelined course measuring 1,360 yards. The holes range in length from 90 yards on the 7th
hole to 200 yards on the 9th. Men's par is 27, Women's is 30. The
course record stands at 25. The tees and greens are both elevated,
making your approach shots difficult. The greens are also very small
so accuracy is most important. The very gentle rolling hills makes it
a pleasurable walk.

33

Pittsburg Golf & Country Club

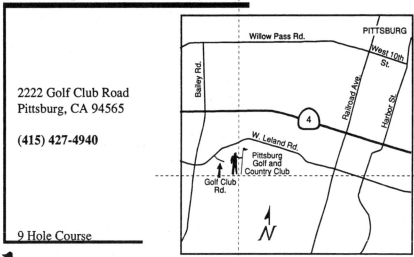

2222 Golf Club Road
Pittsburg, CA 94565

(415) 427-4940

9 Hole Course

1991 Green Fees:

	Weekdays	Weekends
9 Holes:	$8.00	$10.00
18 Holes:	$10.00	$13.00

Twilight Rate: $7.00 / 9 holes and discounted golf car available.
Senior Discount: n.a.

Equipment Rental:

Golf Cars - 9 Holes:	Golf Cars - 18 Holes: $16.00
Pull Carts: $3.00	Clubs: $5.00

Amenities:

Club Pro: n.a.   Lessons: n.a.
A Practice Putting Green, Chipping Green and Driving Range are
available at Pittsburg Golf and Country Club. A Bucket of 30 balls
will run you $1.50. The Restaurant is open from 11 a.m. until 3 p.m.
Mon. thru Sun. Weekend reservations can be made on the prior
Monday, beginning at 7:00 a.m. and for weekdays seven days in
advance. Their busiest day is Saturday, least busy day is Monday.

Course Highlights:

This is a nine hole course with a separate set of tees for playing a
second nine. Total yardage for 18 holes is 6,101 from the Men's
Tees, and is rated 68.8. From the Women's Tees it is 5,869 yards
long and is rated 72.8. Slope is 118. Overall par is 72. The course
record is held by Joe White with a score of 65. This semi-private
course, designed by Alister Mckenzie, opened in 1947. It is considered to be a difficult course, a good test for the low handicap player.
Pittsburg Golf and Country Club regularly hosts the Pittsburg City
Championship Tournament. A new back nine will open sometime
after Labor Day, 1991.

34

San Ramon Royal Vista Golf Club

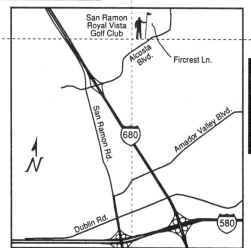

9430 Fircrest Lane
San Ramon, CA 94583

(415) 828-6100

18 Hole Course

1991 Green Fees:

	Weekdays	Weekends
9 Holes:	$8.00	$14.00
18 Holes:	$14.00	$22.00
Twilight Rate:	$8.00	$14.00

Senior Discount: Monthly tickets good Monday - Friday.

Equipment Rental:

Golf Cars - 9 Holes:	$12.00	Golf Cars - 18 Holes:	$18.00
Pull Carts:	$3.00	Clubs:	$12.00

Amenities:

Club Pro: Mark Fleshman   Lessons: $30 / 60 Minutes
A Practice Putting Green, Chipping Green and a Driving Range are available at San Ramon Royal Vista Golf Course. Bucket prices: $2.50 - $4.00. Their restaurant is open from dawn until dark, a cocktail lounge is also available. The Pro Shop carries a complete line of golf equipment. Reservations can be made seven days in advance beginning at day break. Their least busy day is Monday.

Course Highlights:

This Championship 18 hole course first opened under the name of San Ramon National. Located in the valley, the gentle rolling hills and tree lined fairways help make a day of golf an outdoor pleasure. Yardage from the Championship Tees is 6,558, and 6,319 from the Men's. It is rated 70.5 and 69.3, respectively. Yardage from the Women's Tees is 5,793, and is rated 71.4.

35

The Island Club Golf Course

3303 Gateway Road
Bethel Island, CA 94511

(415) 684-2654

18 Hole Course

1991 Green Fees:

	Weekdays	Weekends
9 Holes:	$7.50	n.a.
18 Holes:	$10.00	$13.00

Twilight Rate: At 4:00 p.m. $10.00
Senior Discount: $6.00 - 9 Holes / $8.00 - 18 Holes, weekdays only

Equipment Rental:

Golf Cars - 9 Holes: $11.00   Golf Cars - 18 Holes: $18.00
Pull Carts: $3.00   Clubs: $5.00

Amenities:

Club Pro: Ron Parsons   Lessons: $25 / 30 Minutes
A Practice Putting Green, Chipping Green and Driving Range are
available at The Island Club Golf Course. The cost of a bucket of
practice balls is $2.00. Their restaurant is open from 7 a.m. until 2
p.m., the lounge remains open until 9 p.m. The Pro Shop carries a
full line of golf equipment. Reservations can be made seven days in
advance.

Course Highlights:

This Championship, eighteen hole golf course, previously known as
Bethel Island, is relatively straight except for a few doglegs, the most
severe is located on the 8th hole. Total playing yards from the
Championship Tees is 6,333, rating is 69.4. Yardage from the
Regular Tees is 6,120 and is rated 68.8. From the Women's Tees it
is 5,713 yards long and rated 71.3. Men's par is 72, Women's par is
74. They have planted trees and made other improvements to their
course during the past year.

36

Tilden Park Golf Course

Grizzly Peak Blvd.
& Shasta Road
Alameda, CA 94708

(415) 848-7373

18 Hole Course

Contra Costa County

1991 Green Fees:

	Weekdays	Weekends
9 Holes:	$10.00	$12.00
18 Holes:	$13.00	$17.00
Twilight Rate:	$10.00	

Senior Discount: With membership offer.

Equipment Rental:

Golf Cars - 9 Holes:		Golf Cars - 18 Holes:	$20.00
Pull Carts:	$4.00	Clubs:	$13.00

Amenities:

Club Pro: Paul Wyrybkowski   Lessons: Available
Tilden Park Golf Course offers a Practice Putting Green and a Driving Range. Bucket prices: $1.25 - $2.50. Their Snack Bar is open from 6:30 a.m. until 6:00 p.m. The Pro Shop is fully stocked. Reservations can be made seven days in advance beginning at 6:30 a.m. Their busiest days are Thursdays and Fridays, least busy Mondays and Tuesdays.

Course Highlights:

Tilden Park opened in 1935. For the last seven years it has been operated by the American Golf Corporation. This is a championship 18 hole course. Total yards from the Championship Tees is 6,294; 5,823 from the Men's Tees and from the Women's it is 5,399 yards long. Ratings are: 69.9, 67.8 and 69.7, respectively. Overall par for the course is 70. Tilden Park annually hosts the Bay Regionals. This is a very hilly course, so don't look for too many flat lies. This course is beautiful, well secluded and offers a challenge to all levels of golfers.

37

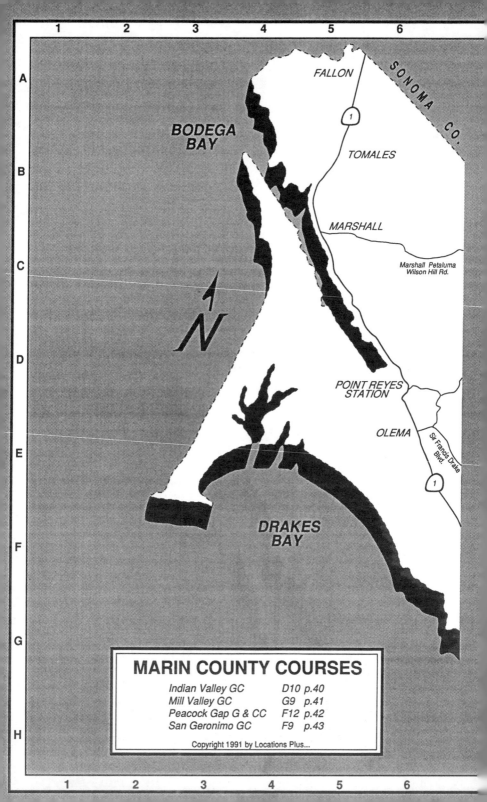

MARIN COUNTY COURSES

Indian Valley GC	D10	p.40
Mill Valley GC	G9	p.41
Peacock Gap G & CC	F12	p.42
San Geronimo GC	F9	p.43

Copyright 1991 by Locations Plus...

Indian Valley Golf Club

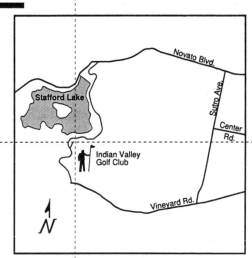

3035 Novato Blvd.
Novato, CA 94948

(415) 897-1118

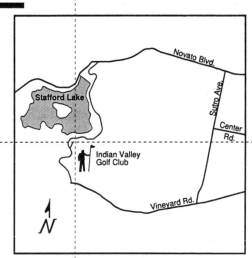

18 Hole Course

1991 Green Fees:

	Weekdays	Weekends
9 Holes:	n.a.	n.a.
18 Holes:	$20.00	$25 Fri. $30.00

Twilight Rate: $15 Wkdys. / $16 Fri. & Holidays / $25 Wknds.
Senior Discount: $15.00 Monday thru Thursday

Equipment Rental:

Golf Cars - 9 Holes: $13.00   Golf Cars - 18 Holes: $20.00
Pull Carts: $3.00   Clubs: $10.00

Amenities:

Club Pro: Ron Hoyt   Lessons: $30 / 30 Minutes
This course offers a Practice Putting Green, Chipping Green and a
Driving Range. Cost of a large bucket is $3.00. Their restaurant and
lounge, "The 19th Hole", is open from 7 a.m. until 4 p.m. The Pro
Shop is complete. Reservations can be made seven days in advance
beginning at 7:00 a.m. Their busiest day of the week is Saturday,
their least busy day is Tuesday.

Course Highlights:

This course is aptly named, Indian Valley, because it uniquely
winds its way through the valley making a complete circle. It is
heavily tree lined, with many rolling fairways. You will encounter
water hazards on eleven of the holes, so having a ball retriever along
would be appropriate. Course ratings are: Women's 70.7, slope 118,
Men's Championship 68.6 and Regular 67.4. Par for the course is 72.
Yardages range from 6,272 from the Championship Tees to 5,304
from the Ladies' Tees.

Mill Valley Golf Course

280 Buena Vista Ave.
Mill Valley, CA 94941

(415) 388-9982

9 Hole Course

1991 Green Fees:

	Weekdays	Weekends
9 Holes:	$7.00	$10.00
18 Holes:	$9.00	$12.00
Twilight Rates:	$5.00	$6.00
Senior Discount:	$5 / 9 holes, $7 / 18 holes	

Equipment Rental:

Golf Cars - 9 Holes: $8.00   Golf Cars - 18 Holes: $14.00
         Pull Carts: $1.50   Clubs: $5.00

Amenities:

Club Pro: Steve Yuhas   Lessons: n.a.

Mill Valley Golf Course offers a Practice Putting Green as their warm-up facility. They have a Snack Bar open daily and a small Pro Shop. Reservations accepted for Tee Times starting before 9:00 a.m., then it is a first come, first serve basis. Golf spikes are required for all golfers.

Course Highlights:

This beautiful, old course opened in 1919. This is a very hilly course sometimes presenting difficult lies. The many mature trees can easily cause problems if you wander off the fairways. It also has a creek running through the course which comes into play on six of the nine holes. The course plays for a total of 4,215 yards from the Men's Tees, is rated 60.6, slope 100. From the Ladies' Tees it is 4,154 yards long and is rated 63.7. Par is 65 / 67. There are no par 5 holes.

41

Peacock Gap Golf & Country Club

333 Biscayne Drive
San Rafael, CA 94901

(415) 453-4940

18 Hole Course

1991 Green Fees:

	Weekdays	Weekends
9 Holes:	n.a.	n.a.
18 Holes:	$24.00	$29.00
Twilight Rate:	$17.00	$22.00
Senior Discount: n.a.		

Equipment Rental:

Golf Cars - 9 Holes: $10.00	Golf Cars - 18 Holes: $20.00
Pull Carts: $3.00	Clubs: $18.00

Amenities:

Club Pro: Al Hand *   Lessons: $35 / 30 Minutes
A Practice Putting Green, Chipping Green and Driving Range are
available at Peacock Gap Golf and Country Club. Bucket prices:
$2.00 - $4.00. Their full restaurant is open 10 - 3 on weekdays, 7 - 3
on weekends. Limited golf accessories are available. *Al Hand is
the Teaching Pro. Weekend reservations can be made on the
Thursday prior at 12 noon, for weekdays, seven days in advance.

Course Highlights:

This semi-private golf course has a par of 71 for the Men, and 72 for
the Women. Course ratings from the Men's Tees, Championship:
69.7, slope 121, Regular: 67.9, slope 118. Ratings from the
Women's Tees, Red: 71.4, slope 114, White: 73.3 - Slope 120. This
is not a terribly long course, yardage from the Championship Tees is
6,284, but don't mistake that to mean that the course is an easy one to
play, even for the experienced golfer.

42

San Geronimo Golf Course

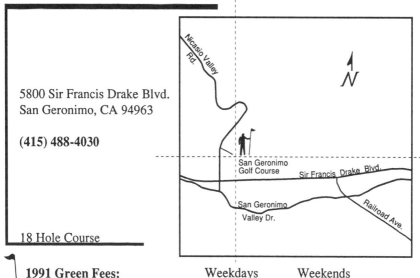

5800 Sir Francis Drake Blvd.
San Geronimo, CA 94963

(415) 488-4030

18 Hole Course

1991 Green Fees:

	Weekdays	Weekends
9 Holes:	$18.00	$23.00
18 Holes:	$35.00	$45.00

Twilight Rates: n.a.
Senior Discount: Club seniors: $15.00 on weekends

Equipment Rental:

Golf Cars - 9 Holes:	Golf Cars - 18 Holes: $22.00
Pull Carts: $4.00	Clubs: $15.00

Amenities:

Club Pro: Doug Talley   Lessons: $30 / Lesson
The San Geronimo Golf Course offers a Practice Putting Green and a
Chipping Green, but no Driving Range. For your convenience, San
Geronimo has a snack bar, full restaurant and lounge. Their Pro
Shop carries a complete line of golf accessories. Reservations can be
made one week in advance.

Course Highlights:

This Championship golf course re-opened in October, 1988 after
being refurbished by architect Robert Muir Graves. This course,
located 20 miles north of San Francisco, surrounded by various
parks, is in a picturesque valley setting. This par 72 course is rated:
Blue 71.9, White 70.6, and Red 73.4. This is a fairly long course,
6,669 yards from the Championship Tees, 6,338 from the White
Tees, and 5,865 from the Ladies' Tees. San Geronimo will permit
you a pleasurable game of golf away from the crowds.

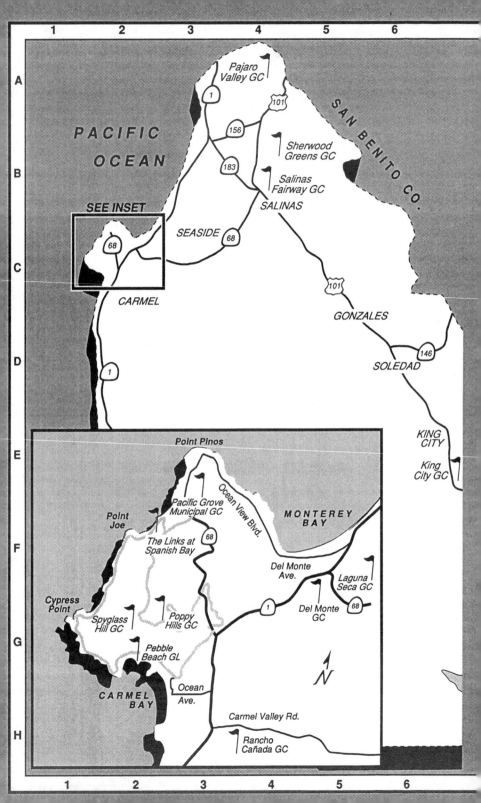

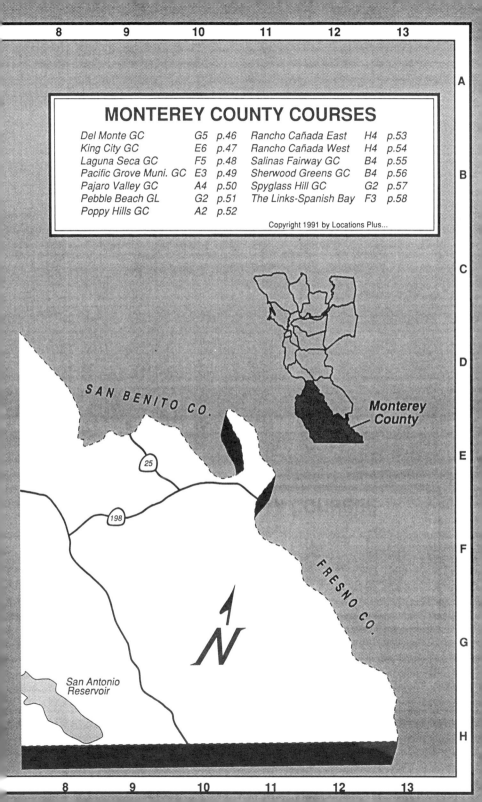

MONTEREY COUNTY COURSES

SAN BENITO CO.

Monterey County

25

198

FRESNO CO.

N

San Antonio Reservoir

Del Monte Golf Course

1300 Sylvan Road
Monterey, CA 93940

(408) 373-2436

18 Hole Course

1991 Green Fees:

	Weekdays	Weekends
9 Holes:	n.a.	n.a.
18 Holes:	$43.00	43.00

Twilight Rate: $10.00 at 200 p.m.
Senior Discount: $20. 7 a.m.-11 a.m. Mon. & Wed. includes golf car

Equipment Rental:

Golf Cars - 9 Holes:	Golf Cars - 18 Holes: $22.00
Pull Carts: $3.00	Clubs: $20.00

Amenities:

Club Pro: Joe Holdridge   Lessons: $20 / 30 Minutes
There is a Practice Putting Green but no Driving Range or Chipping
Green. The Del Monte Bar and Grill is open from 7:30 a.m. to 2:30
p.m. for your convenience. The Pro Shop carries a complete line of
golf accessories. Reservations can be made 60 days in advance.

Course Highlights:

Del Monte Golf Course opened in 1897 and it is believed to be the
oldest golf course west of the Mississippi still in operation on its
original soil. This is a long, and overall, a relatively flat course, but
by no means a beginners. Due to a combination of small greens,
many sandtraps and a great deal of forestry your golfing skills will
often be called upon. Del Monte plays host to the Men's California
State Amateur Tournament, and the Women's California Senior
Amateur Tournament, just to mention a few. Del Monte Golf Course
is one of four courses owned and operated by Pebble Beach Company.

46

King City Golf Course

613 South Vanderhurst Ave.
King City, CA 93930

(408) 385-4546

9 Hole Course

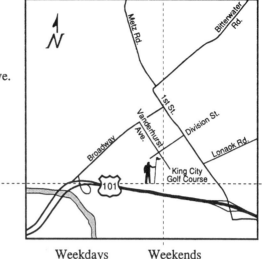

1991 Green Fees:

	Weekdays	Weekends
9 Holes:	$8.00	$9.00
18 Holes:	$10.00	$11.00

Twilight Rate: $5.00 / 9 Holes, $8.00 / 18 Holes, after 2:00 p.m.
Senior Discount: $6.00 / 9 Holes, $11.00 / 18 Holes, weekdays only

Equipment Rental:

Golf Cars - 9 Holes:		Golf Cars - 18 Holes:	$10.00
Pull Carts: $1.00		Clubs: $2.00	

Amenities:

Club Pro: Jon Olson   Lessons: $15 / Lesson
King City Golf Course offers a Practice Putting Green, Chipping
Green and a Driving Range. Bucket prices: $1.25 - $2.50. Their
Snack Bar is open to serve you from 7 a.m. until 7 p.m. Their Pro
Shop is complete. Weekend reservations can be made on the
Monday prior beginning at 7:30 a.m., weekday reservations are not
necessary. Their busiest day is Friday, the least busy day is Monday.

Course Highlights:

King City Golf Course opened in 1953. Since that time, several
modifications have been made to the original layout. Course rating
for the Men is 66.4. The course is 5,634 yards from the White Tees.
Women's rating is 70.3, yardage is 5,350. Par for the course is 70.
The course record is 62. The King City Junior Golf Tournament has
been held here annually since 1957. This course is considered
to be short but challenging.

Monterey County

47

Laguna Seca Golf Club

End of York Road
Monterey, CA 93940

(408) 373-3701

18 Hole Course

Monterey
County

1991 Green Fees:

	Weekdays	Weekends
9 Holes:	n.a.	n.a.
18 Holes:	$40.00	$40.00

Twilight Rate: $19.00 after 2:00 p.m.
Senior Discount: Restricted to Tuesdays with purchase of play card.

Equipment Rental:

Golf Cars - 9 Holes:	Golf Cars - 18 Holes: $22.00
Pull Carts: $3.00	Clubs: $12.00

Amenities:

Club Pro: Dian Murphy   Lessons: $25 / Lesson
Laguna Seca Golf Club offers a Practice Putting Green and a
Chipping Green but no Driving Range. Their new clubhouse,
restaurant and Pro Shop, which opened in February, can more than
fill your needs. Weekend reservations can be made on the prior
Monday beginning at 12:30. They begin taking weekday reservations on the last Friday of the month for the following month.

Course Highlights:

This course, designed by Robert Trent Jones, opened in 1968. It is
located in the hills of the Monterey Peninsula which is known to be
the finest climate area, so the course is referred to as "The Sunshine
Course". This championship course used to play host to the Spalding
Invitational, and now regularly hosts over 200 tournaments a year.
This course offers you all the variety a championship course should,
for instance, plenty of sand, trees, water, hills, and beauty. The
course is rated 70.4 from the Championship Tees, 68.5 from the
regular Tees, Par 71, and 70.2 from the Women's Tees, Par 72. You
will find this course a pleasure to play.

48

Pacific Grove Municipal Golf Course

77 Asilomar Avenue
Pacific Grove, CA 93950

(408) 648-3177

18 Hole Course

1991 Green Fees:

	Weekdays	Weekends
9 Holes:	$9.00	$10.00
18 Holes:	$14.00	$16.00

Twilight Rate: n.a.
Senior Discount: n.a.

Equipment Rental:

Golf Cars - 9 Holes:	Golf Cars - 18 Holes: $19.00
Pull Carts: $2.50	Clubs: $20.00

Amenities:

Club Pro: Peter Vitarisi   Lessons: $25 / 30 Minutes
Pacific Grove Municipal offers a Practice Putting Green and a
Driving Range. Bucket price: $2.00. Their Snack Bar is open from 7
a.m. to 4:30 p.m. for your convenience along with a Pro Shop which
carries a complete line of golf equipment. Weekend reservations can
be made 7 days in advance, Sat. for Sat., etc., beginning at 6:30., for
weekdays 7 days in advance at 6:50 a.m.

Course Highlights:

Pacific Grove Municipal Golf Course originally opened in 1932 as a
9 hole course, but in 1960 it was expanded to include 18. This lovely
old course sits on the tip of scenic Monterey Bay which is reason
enough to ensure an enjoyable golf outing. There is a beautiful old
lighthouse in the middle of the course decorating the the landscape.
The length of the course from the Men's Tees is 5,553 yards, par 70,
while from the Women's Tees it is 5,524 yards with a par of 72.
Make sure to carry along a light jacket in case you encounter some
cool winds off the ocean.

49

Pajaro Valley Golf Club

967 Salinas Road
Watsonville, CA 95076

(408) 724-3851

18 Hole Course

1991 Green Fees:

	Weekdays	Weekends
9 Holes:	n.a.	n.a.
18 Holes:	$32.00	$40.00

Twilight Rate: $19.00
Senior Discount: n.a.

Equipment Rental:

Golf Cars - 9 Holes: Golf Cars - 18 Holes: $22.00
Pull Carts: $3.00 Clubs: $12.00

Amenities:

Club Pro: Nick Lombardo Lessons: $25 / 60 Minutes
There is a Practice Putting Green and a Driving Range available at
Pajaro Valley Golf Club. Bucket prices: $3.00 - $4.00. Their Snack
Bar and lounge is open from 7 a.m. until 4 p.m. Check with the Pro
Shop for information on their Mini-Membership Plan. Reservations
can be made seven days in advance beginning at 7 a.m. This course
is busiest on weekends, least busy on Mondays and Tuesdays.

Course Highlights:

Pajaro Valley Golf Club opened in 1926. It is a beautiful, well
maintained golf course designed for an enjoyable golfing experience
with both pleasurable landscaping as well as a challenging layout.
The course is 6,303 yards long from the Men's Tees and 5,642 yards
from the Women's Tees. Course par is 72. Ratings are, Men's 70.2
and Ladies' 71.0. Pajaro Valley Golf Club regularly hosts the Little
Helpers Golf Tournament.

Pebble Beach Golf Links

Seventeen Mile Drive
Pebble Beach, CA 93953

(408) 624-6611

18 Hole Course

1991 Green Fees: Weekdays   Weekends

	Weekdays	Weekends
9 Holes:	n.a.	n.a.
18 Holes:	$200.00	$200.00

Twilight Rate: Restricted to guests only
Senior Discount: n.a.

Equipment Rental: Golf Car included in Green Fee
   Golf Cars - 9 Holes: Golf Cars - 18 Holes: Included
     Pull Carts: n.a.   Clubs: $35.00

Amenities:

Club Pro: R. J. Harper   Lessons: $40 / 30 Minutes
Pebble Beach offers a Practice Putting Green, Chipping Green and a Driving Range. The Gallery Restaurant offers a wide assortment of food and beverages, they are open from 6 a.m. to 4 p.m. daily. The Pro Shop carries a complete line of golf equipment. The Resort Lodge at Pebble Beach offer their guests a discount on Green Fees. Reservations can only be made one day in advance.

Course Highlights:

This course was designed by Jack Neville and Douglas Grant and was dedicated in 1919. Pebble Beach is one of the four courses owned and operated by the Pebble Beach Company. It is recognized as being one of the finest, most scenic golf courses in the world. It is the annual host to the AT&T Pebble Beach National Pro-Am. In 1992 it will host the U.S. Open Championship. Total yardage from the Championship Tees is 6,799, course rating 75.0. Total yardage from the White Tees is 6,357, course rating 73.0 and total yardage from the Women's Tees is 5,195, course rating 70.3.

Poppy Hills Golf Course

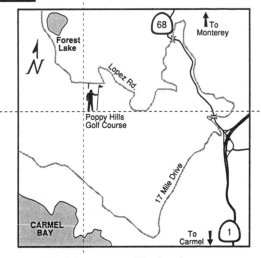

4501 Lopez Road
Pebble Beach, CA 93953

(408) 625-2035

18 Hole Course

1991 Green Fees:	Weekdays	Weekends
9 Holes:	n.a.	n.a.
18 Holes:	$70.00	$70.00

Twilight Rate: n.a.
Senior Discount: n.a.

Equipment Rental:

Golf Cars - 9 Holes:	Golf Cars - 18 Holes: $26.00
Pull Carts: $3.00	Clubs: $25.00

Amenities:

Club Pro: John R. Geertsen   Lessons: $50 / 35 Minutes
Poppy Hills offers a Practice Chipping Green as well as a Driving
Range. Bucket prices: $2.00 - $4.00. For your convenience, Poppy
Hills Restaurant is open from 7 a.m. to 3 p.m. and their Pro Shop
carries a full line of merchandise. Reservations can be made one
month in advance on corresponding day. Their least busy days of the
week are Tuesdays thru Thursdays.

Course Highlights:

The Northern California Golfing Association owns this golf course
which is operated by Poppy Hills, Inc. This course, designed by
Robert Trent Jones, II, opened on June 1, 1986. The setting, on 17
Mile Drive, will be enjoyed as you traverse this long, rolling course.
The course has 3 sets of Tees, the ratings for each are: Blue - 74.6/
slope 141, White - 71.7/slope 134, Red - 71.8/slope 128. The course
record is 67 from the Blue and White Tees. Poppy Hills is host to the
NCGA Amateur events, and in 1991 it will host the NCAA Men's
Golf Championship Tournament and the AT&T National Pebble
Beach Pro-Am. Most golfers will find this a most challenging course
in a naturally beautiful setting.

Rancho Cañada Golf Club - East

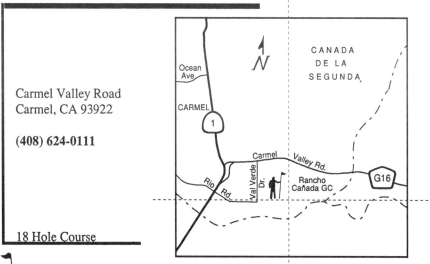

Carmel Valley Road
Carmel, CA 93922

(408) 624-0111

18 Hole Course

1991 Green Fees:	Weekdays	Weekends
9 Holes:	n.a.	n.a.
18 Holes:	$48.00	$48.00

Twilight Rate: $24.00 at 3 p.m. / $10.00 at 5 p.m.
Senior Discount: Yes

Equipment Rental:

Golf Cars - 9 Holes: n.a.   Golf Cars - 18 Holes: $22.00
Pull Carts: $3.00   Clubs: $25.00

Amenities:

Club Pro: Paul "Shim" La Goy   Lessons: $20 / Lesson
Full practice facilities are available. Bucket prices: $2.00 -
$3.00. Their Restaurant and lounge is open from 8 a.m. to 3
p.m., and weekends from 6:30 a.m. until 3:00, closed Mondays.
Their Golf Shop is complete. Weekend reservations can be
made one week in advance beginning at 6:00 a.m. and 30 days in
advance for weekdays.

Course Highlights:

Rancho Cañada - East opened first in 1970. This beautiful Championship Course lies at the foot of the Santa Lucia Mountains and
crosses back and forth over the Carmel River. The East Course
measures 6,434 yards long from the Championship Tees, 6,034 from
the Regular Tees and 5,255 yards from the Women's Tees. Course
ratings are 70.3, 68.7 and 69.0, respectively. Course par is 71 for the
Men and 72 for the Women. Rancho Cañada regularly hosts the
Western States Golf Assoc., The Mexican American Golf Assoc. and
the American and United Airlines Tournaments. You should find
this to be not only a lovely course, but one that tests your golfing
abilities.

Monterey
County

53

Rancho Cañada Golf Club - West

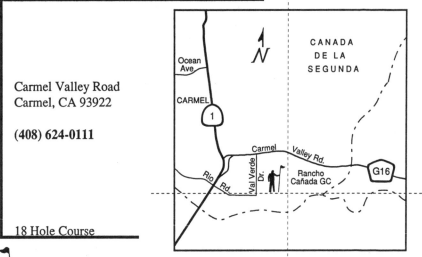

Carmel Valley Road
Carmel, CA 93922

(408) 624-0111

18 Hole Course

1991 Green Fees:

	Weekdays	Weekends
9 Holes:	n.a.	n.a.
18 Holes:	$48.00	$48.00

Twilight Rate: $24.00 at 3:00 p.m. / $10.00 at 5 p.m.
Senior Discount: Yes

Equipment Rental:

Golf Cars - 9 Holes: n.a.	Golf Cars - 18 Holes: $22.00
Pull Carts: $3.00	Clubs: $25.00

Amenities:

Club Pro: Paul "Shim" La Goy   Lessons: $20 / Lesson
Full practice facilities are available. Bucket prices: $2.00 - $3.00.
The Rancho Cañada Restaurant is open on weekdays from 8 a.m.
until 3 p.m., and weekends from 6:30 a.m. until 3:00 p.m., closed
Mondays. Their Golf Shop is complete. Weekend reservations can
be made 7 days in advance beginning at 6 a.m. and for weekdays, 30
days in advance. Busiest on Saturdays, least busy on Tuesdays.

Course Highlights:

Rancho Cañada - West opened in 1971. This Championship course
lies at the foot of the Santa Lucia Mountains and crosses back and
forth over the Carmel River. The West Course is 6,613 yards from
the Championship Tees, 6,142 yards from the Regular Tees and
5,453 yards from the Ladies' Tees. Course ratings are 72.3, 69.5 and
70.5, consecutively. Par is 72 for the Men and 73 for the Women.
Rancho Cañada regularly hosts the Western States Golf Association,
The Mexican American Golf Association, and the American and
United Airlines Tournaments. The fairways you will find a little
narrow, straight shooting is a high priority on this course.

Salinas Fairway Golf Course

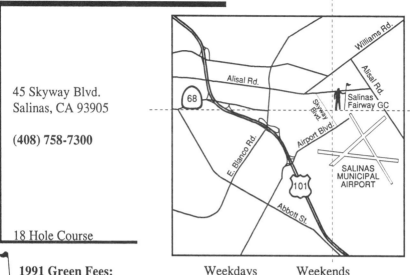

45 Skyway Blvd.
Salinas, CA 93905

(408) 758-7300

18 Hole Course

1991 Green Fees:

	Weekdays	Weekends
9 Holes:	n.a.	n.a.
18 Holes:	$10.00	$12.50

Twilight Rate: $7.50 after 2:30 p.m.
Senior Discount: n.a.

Equipment Rental:

Golf Cars - 9 Holes:	Golf Cars - 18 Holes: $15.00
Pull Carts: $1.50	Clubs: $6.00

Amenities:

Club Pro: Cotton Kaiser   Lessons: $20.00 / Lesson
Salinas Fairway offers a Practice Putting Green, Chipping Green and
a Driving Range. Bucket prices: $1.50 - $2.50. Their Snack Bar is
open from dawn to dusk. The Pro Shop will help in filling your
immediate golfing needs. Reservations for Saturdays can be made
on Mondays prior, and for Sundays on Tuesdays prior. Weekday
reservations are taken one week in advance on Wednesdays.

Course Highlights:

This 18 hole course has been rated 4th among the municipal courses
in the state of California by Golf Digest, which also ranks it number
10 in the United States. Don't be misled by the 111 slope rating, it is
not an easy course. The course is relatively flat, with lateral as well
as directly facing water hazards. Yardage from the Championship
Tees is 6,587, from the Men's Tees it is 6,347 and from the Ladies'
Tees it is 5,674. Ratings are: 69.9, 68.8 and 70.8, respectively. Due
to the increase of the winds each day at around 2:00 p.m., morning
play is recommended unless playing the wind is your strong suit.

Monterey County

55

Sherwood Greens Golf Course

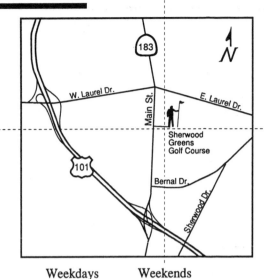

1050 North Main Street
Salinas, CA 93906

(408) 758-7333

9 Hole Course

1991 Green Fees:

	Weekdays	Weekends
9 Holes:	$4.75	$4.75
18 Holes:	$7.50	$7.50

Twilight Rate: n.a.
Senior Discount: n.a.

Equipment Rental:

Golf Cars - 9 Holes:	n.a.	Golf Cars - 18 Holes:	n.a.
Pull Carts:	$1.00	Clubs:	$2.50

Amenities:

Club Pro: Glen Stubblefield   Lessons: $20 / 30 minutes
There is a Practice Putting Green, Chipping Green and a Driving
Range. Bucket prices: $1.75 - $3.00. Residents of Salinas receive a
discount on Green Fees. Reservations are not taken, first come, first
serve.

Course Highlights:

Right in the center of Salina's sporting area lies the Sherwood Greens
9 hole golf course. This is a course you will find easy to walk, no
hills to climb. It is fairly easy to play, good for beginners and for
those who would like to practice with their irons. Except for one par
4 hole, all the rest are par 3's. The shortest hole is 77 yards long, the
longest is 251 yards. Total yardage is 1,249, course par is 28. The
rating for 18 holes is 53.7 and the slope is 72.

56

Spyglass Hill Golf Course

Spyglass Hill Road
 & Stevenson Drive
Pebble Beach, CA 93953

(408) 624-6611

18 Hole Course

1991 Green Fees:

	Weekdays	Weekends
9 Holes:	n.a.	n.a.
18 Holes:	$125.00	$125.00

Twilight Rate: Restricted to guests
Senior Discount: n.a.

Equipment Rental: Golf Car included in Green Fee

Golf Cars - 9 Holes: Golf Cars - 18 Holes: Included
    Pull Carts: n.a.   Clubs: $35.00

Amenities:

Club Pro: Laird Small   Lessons: $40 / 30 Minutes
A Practice Putting Green, Chipping Green and Driving Range are available.   Bucket prices: $2.00 - $4.00.   The Pro Shop is open to help fill your golfing needs.   The Spyglass Grill is open from dawn to dusk serving a wide variety of food and beverages.   Reservations can be made 60 days in advance.

Course Highlights:

Spyglass Hill Golf Course was designed by Robert Trent Jones, Sr., and opened in 1966.   This beautiful course is included in the AT&T Pebble Beach National Pro-Am and has been since 1967.   The first official name was Pebble Beach Pines Golf Club.   The name was changed to honor Robert Louis Stevensons' classic literary work Treasure Island.   Each of the eighteen holes has a title taken from the novel.   The first hole, appropriately named "Treasure Island", has a green completely surrounded by sand creating an island affect. Spyglass Hill is one of four golf courses owned and operated by The Pebble Beach Company.

57

The Links at Spanish Bay

17 Mile Drive
Pebble Beach, CA 93953

(408) 624-6611

18 Hole Course

1991 Green Fees:	Weekdays	Weekends
9 Holes:	n.a.	n.a.
18 Holes:	$125.00	$125.00

Twilight Rate: Restricted to guests
Senior Discount: n.a.

Equipment Rental: Golf Car included in Green Fee
Golf Cars - 9 Holes: Golf Cars - 18 Holes:
   Pull Carts: n.a.   Clubs: $35.00

Amenities:

Club Pro: George Price   Lessons: *
A Practice Putting Green and a Chipping Green are available. The
Clubhouse Bar and Grill is open daily serving a varied assortment of
food and beverages. The Pro Shop carries a complete line of golf
accessories. * Lessons run for 30 minutes and vary in price from $30
with an Assistant Pro to $40 for the Class "A" Pro. Reservations can
be made 60 days in advance.

Course Highlights:

The course was designed by Tom Watson, Robert Trent Jones Jr.,
and Frank "Sandy" Tatum. This is a Scottish style links course,
characterized by rolling fairways and large expanses of sand dunes.
A large portion of the course is exposed to the prevailing winds off
the Pacific Ocean. The inland segment extends through stands of
Monterey pine in the Del Monte Forest, offering a more sheltered
environment. This championship course measures 6,820 yards from
the Blue Tees, 6,078 yards from the White Tees, and 5,287 yards
from the Red Tees. Overall par is 72. The Links at Spanish Bay is
one of the four golf courses owned and operated by the Pebble Beach
Company.

	Fremont	Hayward	Livermore	Monterey	Napa	Novato	Pittsburg	Pleasanton	Oakland	Sacramento	San Francisco	San Jose	San Leandro	Sonoma	Stockton
Fremont		15	30	135	100	80	60	20	40	145	50	35	25	100	65
Hayward	15		30	145	85	60	55	25	20	125	30	40	10	100	70
Livermore	30	30		160	90	90	45	15	50	135	60	45	35	100	40
Monterey	135	145	160		205	180	170	120	140	250	140	80	130	210	200
Napa	100	85	90	205		35	50	75	65	55	75	125	80	20	125
Novato	80	60	90	180	35		60	75	40	90	40	100	50	30	125
Pittsburg	60	55	45	170	50	60		55	40	90	50	90	55	80	45
Pleasanton	20	25	15	120	75	75	55		40	125	45	40	25	90	55
Oakland	40	20	50	140	65	40	40	40		105	10	60	15	80	85
Sacramento	145	125	135	250	55	90	90	125	105		110	170	120	75	65
San Francisco	50	30	60	140	75	40	50	45	10	110		60	20	75	90
San Jose	35	40	45	80	125	100	90	40	60	170	60		50	90	80
San Leandro	25	10	35	130	80	50	55	25	15	120	20	50		140	75
Sonoma	100	100	100	210	20	30	80	90	80	75	90	140	95		135
Stockton	65	70	40	200	125	125	45	55	85	65	90	80	75	135	

Approximate Driving Times (In Minutes) Between Cities in the Bay Area

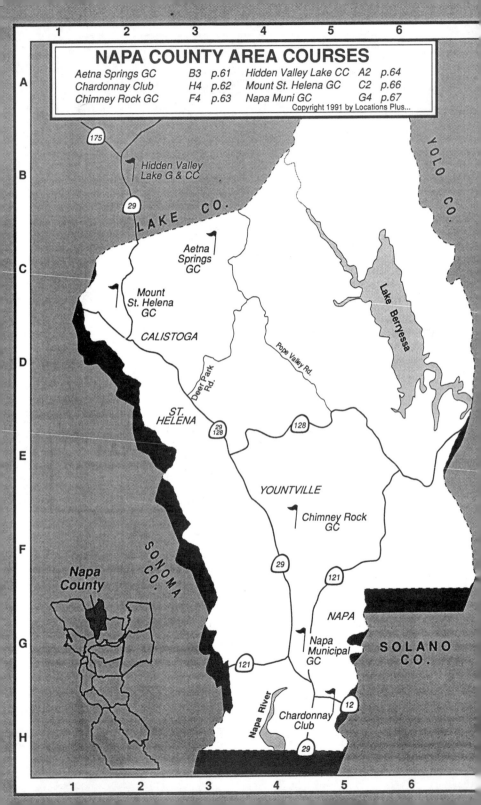

NAPA COUNTY AREA COURSES

Aetna Springs GC	B3	p.61	Hidden Valley Lake CC	A2	p.64
Chardonnay Club	H4	p.62	Mount St. Helena GC	C2	p.66
Chimney Rock GC	F4	p.63	Napa Muni GC	G4	p.67

Aetna Springs Golf Course

1600 Aetna Springs Rd.
Pope Valley, CA 94567

(707) 965-2115

9 Hole Course

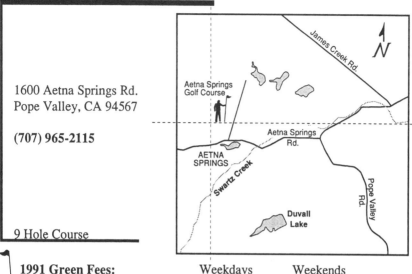

1991 Green Fees:

	Weekdays	Weekends
9 Holes:	$7.00	$8.00
18 Holes:	$7.00	$8.00
Twilight Rate:	$4.00	

Senior Discount: Weekdays only

Equipment Rental:

Golf Cars - 9 Holes: $8.00	Golf Cars - 18 Holes: $15.00
Pull Carts: $1.00	Clubs: $5.00

Amenities:

Club Pro: Kent Stuth   Lessons: $15 / 30 Minutes
There is a new Driving Range at Aetna Springs, the Putting green
will be reopened in the spring of '92. The Snack Shop is open from
dawn to dusk. The Pro Shop is complete. Weekend reservations can
be made on the prior Thursday beginning at 8:00 a.m., for weekdays
one day in advance. Their busiest day of the week is Sunday, least
busy day is Tuesday.

Course Highlights:

Aetna Springs Golf Course is one of the oldest courses in the west. It
opened in the late 1890's as part of the Aetna Springs Resort. In the
1920's it was expanded to a full 9 holes and at that time became a
public course. Total yardage from the Men's Tees is 2,686 and 2,527
from the Women's Tees. Par for 9 holes is 35. Six of the holes are
par 4's with 2 par 3's and 1 par 5. Course Rating is 64.7. The course
has been upgraded to provide challenging play for both the beginner
and the experienced player. The sights are beautiful in the wooded
Pope Valley setting.

Napa
County

Chardonnay Club

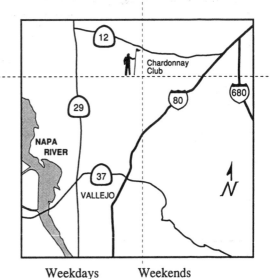

2555 Jameson Canyon Rd.
(California Highway 12)
Napa, CA 94558

(707) 257-8950

27 Hole Course

1991 Green Fees:

	Weekdays	Weekends
9 Holes:	$40.00	$40.00
18 Holes:	$40.00	$50.00
Twilight Rates:	$25.00	$30.00
Senior Discount: n.a.		

Equipment Rental: Golf Car included in Green Fee
Golf Cars - 9 Holes: Golf Cars - 18 Holes:
       Pull Carts: n.a.   Clubs: $15.00

Amenities:
Club Pro: Mike Cook   Lessons: *Available
Promoting a Country Club atmosphere, all their warm-up facilities, including their driving range are included in the Green Fees. Complete dining facilities are available. The Pro Shop carries a full line of golf accessories. *For more information on golf lessons, contact the Pro Shop. Reservations can be made two weeks in advance.

Course Highlights:
Chardonnay is a unique Scottish design course set in the wine country of California. The 27 holes represent three 18 hole golf courses in one. Yardage will range from 5,000 to 7,100. There are 5 separate teeing areas to accommodate every experience level of golfer. The landscape is varied to include wooded areas, ponds, streams and the occasional open fairway that appeals to most golfers. A day at Chardonnay should prove to be most enjoyable.

62

Chimney Rock Golf Course

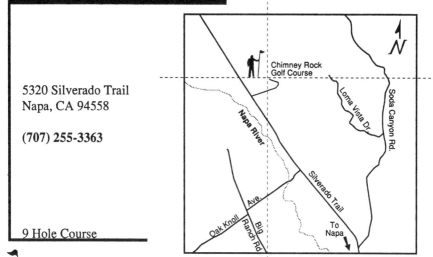

5320 Silverado Trail
Napa, CA 94558

(707) 255-3363

9 Hole Course

1991 Green Fees:

	Weekdays	Weekends
9 Holes:	$12.00	$15.00
18 Holes:	$16.00	$20.00

Twilight Rate: Same as 9 hole fees.
Senior Discount: $6.50 Monday through Friday

Equipment Rental:

Golf Cars - 9 Holes:	Golf Cars - 18 Holes: $16.00
Pull Carts: $2.50	Clubs: $15.00

Amenities:

Club Pro: n.a.   Lessons: n.a.
A Practice Putting Green is available, but no Chipping Green or
Driving Range. The Chimney Rock Coffee Shop is open from 6 a.m.
until 9 p.m. for your convenience. The Pro Shop will help you in
selecting merchandise to fill your golfing needs. Reservations can be
made two weeks in advance. Reservations for more than 4 people
requires a $5.00 deposit per person.

Course Highlights:

This is a 9 hole championship golf course set in the beautiful wine
country of Napa Valley. There is water directly in front of you as
you tee off on two of the holes. The other hazards on the course are
less threatening. You will find the greens here are fast and consis-
tent. Par for 9 holes is 36. Yardage from the Championship Tees is
3,484, Men's yardage is 3,386 and Women's' yardage is 2,935. You
will play two par 5 holes, two par 3 holes with the remainder being
par 4's.

63

Hidden Valley Lake Golf & Country Club

#1 Hartman Rd.
Middletown, CA 95461

(707) 987-3035

18 Hole Course

Hidden Valley Lake
Golf & Country Club

1991 Green Fees:

	Weekdays	Weekends
9 Holes:	$10.00	$15.00
18 Holes:	$15.00	$22.00

Twilight Rates: $6.00 after 2:30 weekdays / special golf car rate
Senior Discount: $3.00 less, Monday - Thursday

Equipment Rental:

Golf Cars - 9 Holes: $12.00	Golf Cars - 18 Holes: $18 / $20
Pull Carts: $2.00	Clubs: $8.00

Amenities:

Club Pro: Rob Kenny   Lessons: $20 / 30 Minutes
This course offers a Practice Putting Green and a Driving Range.
Their full restaurant and lounge is open from 7 a.m. until 5 p.m.
daily. The Pro Shop offers a nice selection of golf equipment.
Reservations can be made one week in advance. Their busiest
day of the week is Saturday, least busy day is Thursday.

Course Highlights:

This 18 hole course was built in 1968 as part of the Boise-Cascade
subdivision. They have recently completed construction of men's tee
boxes. The front 9 holes are flat and long. The back 9 holes are
more picturesque as the course becomes hilly and additional trees
line the fairways. You have an opportunity on 10 of the 18 holes to
submerge your ball in a crossing creek or pond. The 15th hole offers
a spectacular view of the valley from the 150 foot elevated tee area.
Course yardages range from 6,590 to 5,593. Men's par is 72,
Women's is 74. This course hosts the Hidden Valley Lake Pro-Am,
and the Pacific Women's Golf Assoc. Team Championship.

64

Mount St. Helena Golf Course

2025 Grant Street
Calistoga, CA 94515

(707) 942-9966

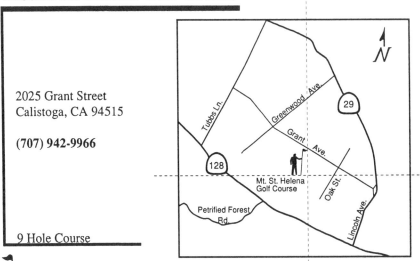

9 Hole Course

1991 Green Fees:

		Weekdays	Weekends
9 Holes:		$8.00	$10.00
18 Holes:		$8.00	$10.00
Twilight Rate:	After 4:00 p.m.	$4.00	$5.00
Senior Discount:	$6.00 - all day		

Equipment Rental:

Golf Cars - 9 Holes: Golf Cars - 18 Holes: $14.00
    Pull Carts: $2.00   Clubs: $5.00

Amenities:

Club Pro: n.a.   Lessons: n.a.
This 9 hole course offers a Practice Putting Green, but no Chipping
Green or Driving Range. The Snack Shop is open from dawn to dusk
for your convenience. The Pro Shop will help fill your immediate
golfing needs. They do not take reservations in advance, first come,
first serve.

Course Highlights:

Mount St. Helena Golf Course is located in scenic Napa Valley.
Overall par for the course is 68. Total yardage from the Men's Tees
is 5,420, and 5,250 yards from the Women's Tees. There are only
two par 3 holes on the course, the rest are par 4's. There are sufficient variations on this flat, easy to walk, course. There are plenty
of trees and narrow fairways to test your golfing abilities.

Napa County

65

Napa Municipal Golf Course

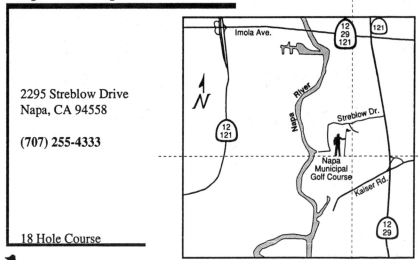

2295 Streblow Drive
Napa, CA 94558

(707) 255-4333

18 Hole Course

1991 Green Fees:

	Weekdays	Weekends
9 Holes:	n.a.	n.a.
18 Holes:	$11.00	$17.00
Twilight Rates:	$7.00	$8.00

Senior Discount: Napa City residents only.

Equipment Rental:

Golf Cars - 9 Holes:	Golf Cars - 18 Holes: $17.00
Pull Carts: $3.00	Clubs: $15.00

Amenities:

Club Pro: Bob Swan   Lessons: $22.50 / 30 Minutes
Napa Municipal Golf Course offers a Practice Putting Green and a
Driving Range. Bucket prices: $1.50 - $3.00. The Out of Bounds
Restaurant is open daily for your convenience. The Pro Shop carries
a complete line of golf accessories. Reservations can be made seven
days in advance by phone beginning at 7:00 a.m. This course is
busiest on weekends, and least busy on Thursdays.

Course Highlights:

This course opened in May of 1967. It is the qualifying site for
Kaiser, Anheuser-Busch Tour Tournaments. Total yardage from the
Blue Tees is 6,730, from the White Tees it is 6,506, and 5,956 from
the Red Tees. It is rated 71.7, 70.7 and 73.6, respectively. Course
par is 72 / 73. On 13 of the holes you will encounter a water hazard
either alongside or crossing the fairways. A number of the doglegs
are rather severe. This course is nick-named "JFK" and "Kennedy"
because of its location in the John F. Kennedy Park.

Quantity Discounts Available!

For club tournaments or company golf outings the <u>Bay Area Golf Guide</u> makes a perfect gift.

Call or write for details of the attractive discounts available to your group or organization.

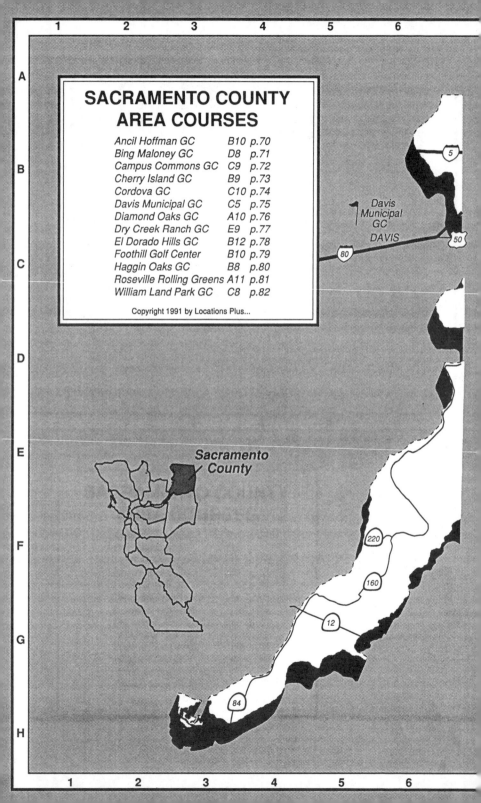

SACRAMENTO COUNTY
AREA COURSES

Ancil Hoffman GC	*B10*	*p.70*
Bing Maloney GC	*D8*	*p.71*
Campus Commons GC	*C9*	*p.72*
Cherry Island GC	*B9*	*p.73*
Cordova GC	*C10*	*p.74*
Davis Municipal GC	*C5*	*p.75*
Diamond Oaks GC	*A10*	*p.76*
Dry Creek Ranch GC	*E9*	*p.77*
El Dorado Hills GC	*B12*	*p.78*
Foothill Golf Center	*B10*	*p.79*
Haggin Oaks GC	*B8*	*p.80*
Roseville Rolling Greens	*A11*	*p.81*
William Land Park GC	*C8*	*p.82*

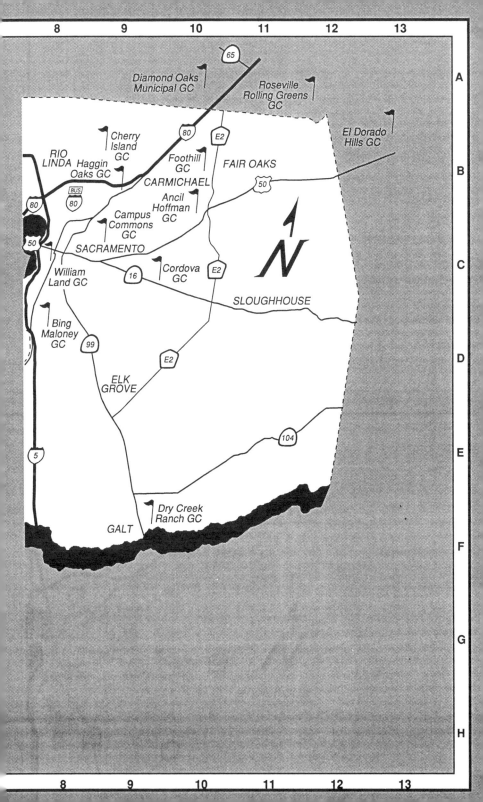

Ancil Hoffman Golf Course

6700 Tarshes Dr.
Carmichael, CA

(916) 482-5660

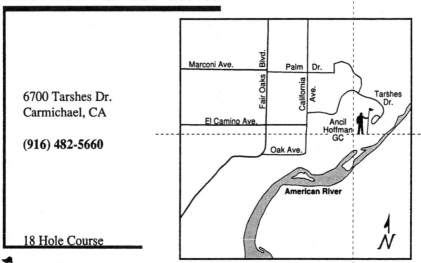

18 Hole Course

1991 Green Fees:

	Weekdays	Weekends
9 Holes:	$8.00	$9.00
18 Holes:	$13.00	$15.00
Twilight Rate:	$8.00	$9.00

Senior Discount: $8.50 weekdays with senior card

Equipment Rental:

Golf Cars- 9 Holes:	$9.00	Golf Cars - 18 Holes:	$16.00
Pull Carts:	$2.00	Clubs:	$10.00

Amenities:

Club Pro: Steve Price   Lessons: $25 / 30 Minutes
This course offers a Practice Putting Green and a Driving Range.
Bucket prices: $2.00 - $4.00. They have a Snack Bar open from
dawn to dusk, and a cocktail lounge for your convenience. The Pro
Shop carries a large inventory of golf equipment. Reservations for
Tee Times during the week can be made 7 days in advance. For the
weekends, on Monday morings prior, beginning at 6:30.

Course Highlights:

This public, 18 hole course has been in operation for the past 25
years. It is truly a challenging course with narrow fairways, and
contoured greens. The mature trees will cause great difficulty to the
golfer who wanders off the fairways. The course offers three sets of
tees. Par of the course is 72, course record stands at 63.

Bing Maloney Golf Course

6801 Freeport Blvd.
Sacramento, CA 95822

(916) 428-9401

18 Hole Course

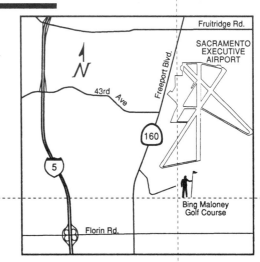

1991 Green Fees:

	Weekday	Weekends
9 Holes:	$7.00	$8.00
18 Holes:	$11.50	$14.00
Twilight Rate:	$7.00	$8.00

Senior Discount: $8.00

Equipment Rental:

Golf Cars - 9 Holes: $8.00   Golf Cars - 18 Holes: $16.00
Pull Carts: $2.00   Clubs: $10.00

Amenities:

Club Pro: Tom E. Doris   Lessons: $25 / Lesson
This course offers a Practice Putting Green and a Driving Range.
Bucket prices: $2.00 - $3.50. They provide a full restaurant that
is open from dawn to dusk and a Pro Shop with an extensive
inventory of golf equipment. Reservations can be made one
week in advance. Their busiest day of the week is Saturday,
least busy day is Tuesday.

Course Highlights:

This busy 18 hole course, where over 100,000 rounds of golf are
played each year, opened in 1952. The course measures 6,281 yards
from the Championship Tees, is rated 69.7 and par is 72. From the
Ladies' Tees it is 5,972 yards long, rated 72.6, slope 119 and par is
73. The course is flat so your lies will be good provided you stay
within the narrow fairways. The small greens insist upon accurate
approach shots. Water can only slow you down on one hole.

Sacramento County

71

Campus Commons Golf Course

2 Cadillac Drive
Sacramento, CA 95825

(916) 922-5861

9 Hole Course

1991 Green Fees:

	Weekdays	Weekends
9 Holes:	$6.00	$6.50
18 Holes:	$10.00	$10.50

Twilight Rate: n.a.
Senior Discount: n.a.

Equipment Rental:

Golf Cars- 9 Holes: $8.00   Golf Cars - 18 Holes:
Pull Carts: $1.00   Clubs: $5.00

Amenities:

Club Pro: Ray Arinno   Lessons: Yes
There is a only a Practice Putting Green here at Campus Commons
Golf Course. The club house contains a small Snack Bar along with
a Pro Shop. Group and private lessons are available and are taught
by Mike Fraccolli. Reservations can be made one week in advance.
Their busiest day of the week is Sunday.

Course Highlights:

This 9 hole, par 3 course sits on the bank of the American River. It
has been in operation for the past 19 years. The Men's rating is 54,
the Ladies' is 56. Total yardage from the Men's Tees is 1,673, from
the Ladies' it is 1,508. Par for the course is 29.

Cherry Island Golf Course

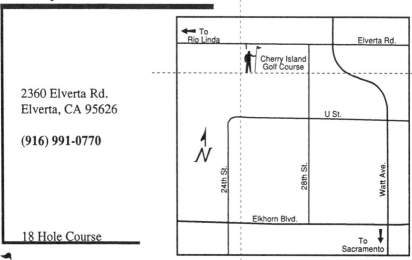

2360 Elverta Rd.
Elverta, CA 95626

(916) 991-0770

18 Hole Course

1991 Green Fees:

	Weekday	Weekends
9 Holes:	$8.00	$9.00
18 Holes:	$13.00	$15.00
Twilight Rate:	$8.00	$9.00

Senior Discount: $8.50 with Sr. Resident Card

Equipment Rental:

Golf Cars - 9 Holes: $9.00   Golf Cars - 18 Holes: $16.00
Pull Carts: $3.00   Clubs: $10.00

Amenities:

Club Pro: Blair Kline   Lessons: $25 / Lesson
Cherry Island offers a Practice Putting Green, Chipping Green and a Driving Range. Bucket prices: $2.00 - $4.00. They provide a full restaurant and lounge and a Pro Shop which carries an extensive inventory of golf equipment. Reservations can be made one week in advance for weekday Tee Times and on the Monday prior for the weekends.

Course Highlights:

This new, 18 hole, championship course opened in June of 1990 and is a lovely addition to the area. Designed by Robert Muir Graves, it features water hazards, mature Oak trees, rolling Bentgrass greens and Bluegrass fairways. There are four sets of tees, Blue, White, Gold and Red. The yardages are 6,562, 6,201, 5,556 and 5,163, respectively. Overall par is 72.

Sacramento County

Cordova Golf Course

9425 Jackson Rd.
Sacramento, CA 95826

(916) 362-1196

18 Hole Course

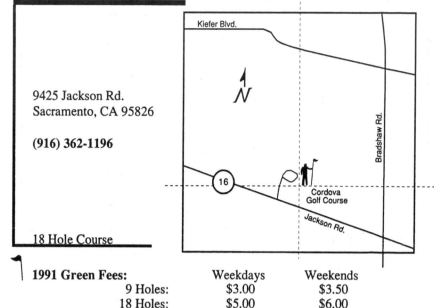

1991 Green Fees:

	Weekdays	Weekends
9 Holes:	$3.00	$3.50
18 Holes:	$5.00	$6.00

Twilight Rate: Less 20%
Senior Discount: n.a.

Equipment Rental:

Golf Cars- 9 Holes: $6.00   Golf Cars - 18 Holes: $12.00
    Pull Carts: $2.00   Clubs: $6.00

Amenities:

Club Pro: Jim Marta   Lessons: $25.00
There is a Practice Putting Green and Driving Range available at
Cordova Golf Course. Bucket prices: $2.00 - $3.00. There is a
Snack Bar open from 7 a.m. until 8 p.m. for your convenience. A
complete Pro Shop is also available. Reservations can be made one
week in advance. Their least busy day is Monday. The Driving
Range is open till 10:00 p.m. March thru November.

Course Highlights:

Cordova Golf Course is a short 18 hole course that measures 4,755
yards from the Men's Tees and 4,728 from the Ladies'. Par for the
Men is 63, it is rated 61, slope is 90. Ladies' Par is 66, rated 64.9,
slope is 96. The course is flat making it easy to walk. The greens are
small and the fairways, lined with plenty of trees, are narrow. You
will encounter water on three of the holes. The course is not difficult. There is only 1 par 5 hole, 7 par 4 holes and 10 par 3 holes.
Good beginners course.

Sacramento County

74

Davis Municipal Golf Course

Rd. 29, Hwy. 113
Davis, CA 95617

(916) 756-4010

18 Hole Course

1991 Green Fees:

	Weekday	Weekends
9 Holes:	n.a.	n.a.
18 Holes:	$9.00	$9.00

Twilight Rate: $6.00
Senior Discount: $6.00 weekdays only

Equipment Rental:

Golf Cars - 9 Holes: n.a.   Golf Cars - 18 Holes: $15.00
Pull Carts: $1.50   Clubs: $4.00 / $7.00

Amenities:

Club Pro: Jerry Lilliedall   Lessons: $20 / 30 Minutes
Davis Golf Course provides two Practice Putting Greens and a
Driving Range. Bucket prices: $1.50 - $3.00. They have a Snack
Bar open from dawn until dusk. The Pro Shop will be able to meet
most of your golfing needs. Reservations can be made one week in
advance.

Course Highlights:

Davis Golf Course is a nice, easy to play, and easy to walk, 18 hole
golf course. The course is 4,998 yards long from the Men's Tees
and is rated 63.4. From the Ladies' Tees it is 4,445 yards long and
rated 60.9. There are no par 5 holes, and 6 of the holes are par 3's.
Par for the course is 66 / 67. Course record stands at 56. The course
is flat and the fairways are tree lined. There are two fairway water
hazards to be negotiated. Most of the course is surrounded by farm
land.

75

Diamond Oaks Municipal Golf Course

1000 Diamond Oaks Rd.
Roseville, CA 95678

(916) 783-4947

18 Hole Course

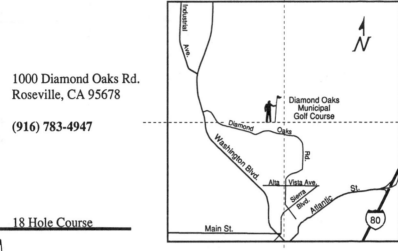

1991 Green Fees:

	Weekdays	Weekends
9 Holes:	$5.50	$6.00
18 Holes:	$9.00	$10.00

Twilight Rate: $4.50
Senior Discount: Residents of Roseville only.

Equipment Rental:

Golf Cars- 9 Holes: $8.00   Golf Cars - 18 Holes: $16.00
Pull Carts: $1.00 / $1.25   Clubs: $5.00 / $10.00

Amenities:

Club Pro: Ed Vasconcellos   Lessons: $25 / 30 Minutes
There are two Practice Putting Greens and a Driving Range available. Bucket prices: $1.50 - $3.00. They provide a full restaurant and a Snack Bar, open from dawn to dusk. Their new Pro Shop carries an extensive inventory of golf equipment. Reservations can be made one week in advance for weekdays, and on Monday prior, beginning at 7 a.m. by phone, or 6:45 a.m. in person, for weekends.

Course Highlights:

This public, 18 hole, golf course opened in 1963. It is a lovely rolling course with plenty of Oak trees lining the wide, forgiving fairways. It presents a challenge to every level of golfer. The course measures 6,283 yards from the Championship Tees, 6,065 from the Men's Tees and 5,608 from the Ladies'. Par for the course is 72 / 73.

76

Dry Creek Ranch Golf Course

809 Crystal Way
Galt, CA 95632

(209) 745-2330

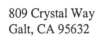

18 Hole Course

1991 Green Fees:

	Weekday	Weekends
9 Holes:	$7.00	$12.00
18 Holes:	$14.00	$24.00

Twilight Rate: n.a.
Senior Discount: n.a.

Equipment Rental:

Golf Cars - 9 Holes: $9.00	Golf Cars - 18 Holes: $18.00
Pull Carts: $2.00	Clubs: $10.00

Amenities:

Club Pro: Rod Sims   Lessons: $20

A Practice Putting Green and a Driving Range are available. Bucket price ranges from $1.25 to $2.00 Their Snack Bar is open from 9 a.m. until 9 p.m.   Their full restaurant "Golden Acorn" is also available. The Pro Shop carries an extensive inventory of golf equipment to help fill your golfing needs. You can reserve Tee Times two weeks in advance.

Course Highlights:

This busy 18 hole course, designed by Jack Fleming, opened in 1962. It is in excellent condition. Recently they extended 5 of their "T" Boxes for the Blue Tees. There are towering Oak trees throughout the course. Be sure to bring your ball retriever for there are plenty of water holes, the name of the course, "Dry Creek Ranch", is deceiving.

Sacramento County

77

El Dorado Hills Golf Course

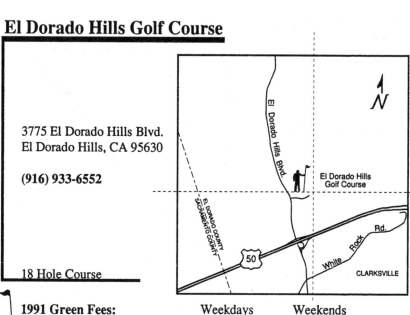

3775 El Dorado Hills Blvd.
El Dorado Hills, CA 95630

(916) 933-6552

18 Hole Course

1991 Green Fees:

	Weekdays	Weekends
9 Holes:	$9.00	$12.00
18 Holes:	$16.00	$20.00

Twilight Rate: $4.00
Senior Discount: Monthly passes

Equipment Rental:

Golf Cars- 9 Holes: $10 / $12   Golf Cars - 18 Holes: $16 / $18
Pull Carts: $3 / 9 Holes   Clubs: $5.00

Amenities:

Club Pro: Ted Fitzpatrick   Lessons: $20 / 30 Minutes
El Dorado Hills provides a Practice Putting Green, Chipping Green
and a Driving Range. Bucket prices: $1.50 - $3.00. Their Snack
Bar, which features a great breakfast, is open from 5 a.m. until 10
p.m. The Pro Shop can fill your immediate golfing needs. Weekend
reservations can be made seven days in advance, weekday reservations can be made two weeks ahead.

Course Highlights:

This eighteen hole course, designed by Robert Trent, Sr., has been in
operation since 1962. This is a short 18 hole course. From the
White Tees it plays for a total of 4,233 yards and is rated 58.3, slope
is 93. Par for the course is 61, course record stands at 54. The
course is hilly and has plenty of trees. There are water hazards on 11
of the holes, so bring along a few extra balls. This is a difficult
course, a test of your golfing abilities. This course hosts over 400
tournaments a year.

Foothill Golf Center

7000 Verner Ave.
Sacramento, CA 95841

(916) 725-3355

9 Hole Course

1991 Green Fees:

	Weekday	Weekends
9 Holes:	$4.25	$4.75
18 Holes:	$7.75	$8.50

Twilight Rate: n.a.
Senior Discount: n.a.

Equipment Rental:

Golf Cars - 9 Holes: n.a.   Golf Cars - 18 Holes: n.a.
       Pull Carts: $1.25   Clubs: $2.50

Amenities:

Club Pro: Paul Ottaviano   Lessons: $20 / 45 Minutes
Foothill Golf Center provides a Practice Putting Green and a Chipping Green. Their restaurant is open daily from dawn to dusk. Their Pro Shop carries a limited amount of golf merchandise. They do not take advance reservations.

Course Highlights:

This is a true, 9 hole, beginners course. It is the smallest course in Sacramento. The longest hole is 148 yards, the average hole length is 120 yards. If you are just learning to play the game of golf, and you do not want to be bothered by hazards of any kind, then this is the course for you.

Sacramento County

79

Haggin Oaks Municipal Golf Course

3645 Fulton Ave.
Sacramento, CA 95821

(916) 481-4507

2 - 18 Hole Courses

1991 Green Fees:

	Weekdays	Weekends
9 Holes:	$5.75	$7.00
18 Holes:	$11.50	$14.00

Twilight Rate: $7.00
Senior Discount: $9.25 for residents of Sacramento

Equipment Rental:

Golf Cars- 9 Holes: $8.00	Golf Cars - 18 Holes: $16.00
Pull Carts: $2.00	Clubs: $7.50

Amenities:

Club Pro: Ken Morton   Lessons: $30 / 30 Minutes
Haggin Oaks offers a Practice Putting Green, a Chipping Green and a
Driving Range. Bucket prices: $2.00 - $3.50. They have a Snack
Bar that is open from dawn to dusk and a large Pro Shop for your
convenience. Reservations can be made for the weekends by calling
on the Tuesday morning prior and weekday reservations can be made
one week in advance.

Course Highlights:

Haggin Oaks Golf Course consists of two 18 hole courses. The
North Course designed by Alister Mckenzie in 1957-1959, and the
South Course designed by Mike McDonough in 1932. The courses
are fairly flat, the fairways are lined by mature trees. The greens are
of average size. Arcade Creek winds its way throughout the course.
The South Course measures 6,287 yards and is rated 69.1. The North
Course, the championship course, measures 6,860 yards and is rated
71.4. Par for both courses is 72. The record low score for the South
Course is 63 and for the North Course it is 64. This is a great value
facility.

Roseville Rolling Greens Golf Course

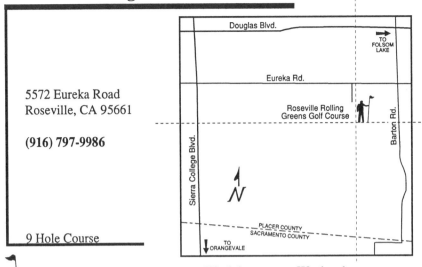

5572 Eureka Road
Roseville, CA 95661

(916) 797-9986

9 Hole Course

1991 Green Fees:

	Weekday	Weekends
9 Holes:	$6.00	$7.00
18 Holes:	$10.00	$12.00

Twilight Rate: n.a.
Senior Discount: n.a.

Equipment Rental:

Golf Cars - 9 Holes: n.a.	Golf Cars - 18 Holes: n.a.
Pull Carts: $1.00	Clubs: n.a.

Amenities:

Club Pro: Lessons: Available
Roseville Rolling Greens offers a Practice Putting Green as their warm-up facility. They have a Snack Bar open from dawn to dusk and a small Pro Shop. The course does not take reservations, first come, first serve. If you are interested in golf lessons, please contact the Pro Shop.

Course Highlights:

This executive 9 hole course has been open for the past 40 years. It is a busy course, difficult, but pleasant to play. The course features plenty of sand traps, trees and water hazards. The name "Rolling Greens" best describes the terrain. Total yardage is 1,500, par is 27. Course records are 24 for 9 holes and 50 for 18 holes.

81

William Land Park Golf Course

1701 Sutterville Rd.
Sacramento, CA 95831

(916) 455-5014

9 Hole Course

1991 Green Fees:

	Weekdays	Weekends
9 Holes:	$5.75	$7.00
18 Holes:		

Twilight Rate: n.a.
Senior Discount: $4.25

Equipment Rental:

Golf Cars- 9 Holes: n.a.	Golf Cars - 18 Holes: n.a.
Pull Carts: $1.00	Clubs: $5.00

Amenities:

Club Pro: Fred Crockett   Lessons: $25 / Lesson
William Land Park Golf Course offers a Practice Putting Green and a Chipping Green as warm-up facilities. Their Snack Bar is open from dawn to dusk. The Pro Shop can meet most of your golfing needs. Reservations can be made one week in advance. Their busiest day of the week is Saturday, least busy day is Tuesday.

Course Highlights:

This nine hole course has been in operation since 1929. It is a well matured course with lots of big trees lining the fairways. The big greens give an advantage to the golfer who's approach shots are not yet perfected. Course record stands at 59.

Sacramento County

82

	Fremont	Hayward	Livermore	Monterey	Napa	Novato	Pittsburg	Pleasanton	Oakland	Sacramento	San Francisco	San Jose	San Leandro	Sonoma	Stockton
Fremont		11	20	103	82	62	45	16	32	110	36	26	19	77	49
Hayward	11		25	110	66	48	42	20	16	95	23	32	6	75	54
Livermore	20	25		123	67	67	35	12	38	103	44	33	28	75	29
Monterey	103	110	123		158	138	131	91	108	193	109	61	99	162	152
Napa	82	66	67	158		28	39	56	50	41	56	97	61	15	96
Novato	62	48	67	138	28		46	57	30	69	29	76	40	23	96
Pittsburg	45	42	35	131	39	46		41	31	71	37	70	41	63	35
Pleasanton	16	20	12	91	56	57	41		29	97	36	30	19	69	41
Oakland	32	16	38	108	50	30	31	29		82	6	47	11	61	64
Sacramento	110	95	103	193	41	69	71	97	82		84	132	93	56	50
San Francisco	36	23	44	109	56	29	37	36	6	84		48	17	67	70
San Jose	26	32	33	61	97	76	70	30	47	132	48		38	108	62
San Leandro	19	6	28	99	61	40	41	19	11	93	17	38		72	57
Sonoma	77	75	75	162	15	23	63	69	61	56	67	108	72		104
Stockton	49	54	29	152	96	96	35	41	64	50	70	62	57	104	

Approximate Miles Between Cities in Bay Area

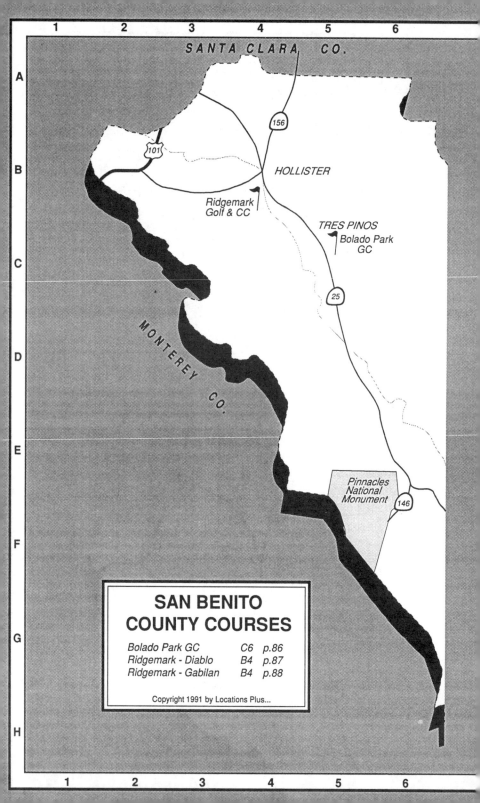

SAN BENITO
COUNTY COURSES

Bolado Park GC	*C6*	*p.86*
Ridgemark - Diablo	*B4*	*p.87*
Ridgemark - Gabilan	*B4*	*p.88*

Copyright 1991 by Locations Plus...

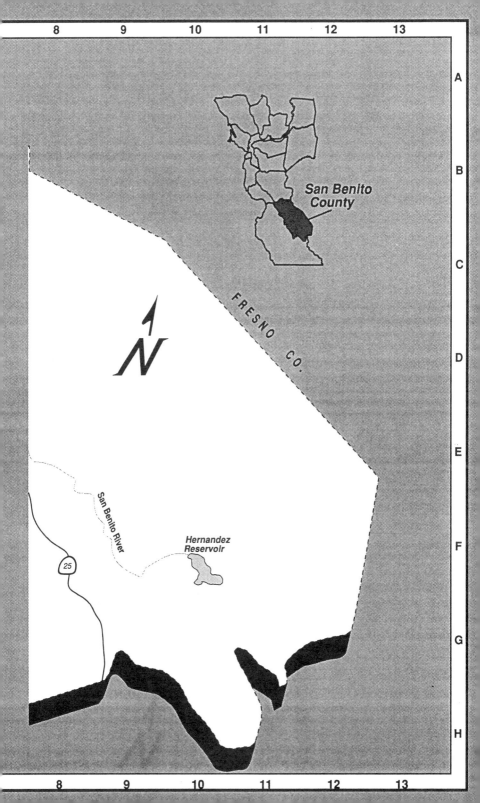

Bolado Park Golf Course

7777 Airline Highway
Tres Pinos, CA 95075

(408) 628-9995

9 Hole Course

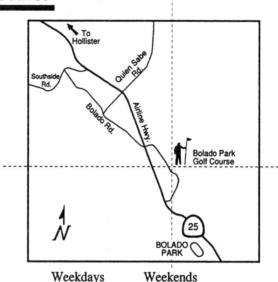

1991 Green Fees:

	Weekdays	Weekends
9 Holes:	$8.00	$12.00
18 Holes:	$8.00	$12.00
Twilight Rate: After 3 p.m.	$6.00	$10.00

Senior Discount: $6.00 - Monday, Thursday & Friday

Equipment Rental:

Golf Cars - 9 Holes:	Golf Cars - 18 Holes: $18.00
Pull Carts: $2.00	Clubs: $2.00

Amenities:

Club Pro: Bob Trevino   Lessons: $20 / 30 Minutes*
Bolado Park Golf Course offers a Practice Putting Green and a
Driving Range. Bucket prices: $1.50 - $2.50. The Snack Bar is open
from 7 a.m. until 7 p.m. The Pro Shop will help you fill most of your
golfing needs. *Teaching pro is Lary Philbrick. They do not take
reservations, first come, first serve.

Course Highlights:

This well maintained, nine hole, course has a separate set of tees for
playing a second nine. Total yardage for 18 holes is 5,986 from the
Men's Tees and 5,636 yards from the Ladies' Tees. Course ratings
are 67.5 and 71.5, respectively. Par for the course is 70. It is a full
nine holes with all the features you would expect to find on a
regulation 18 hole course. The fairways are lined by many large
trees making it difficult to cross over to another hole. It is a lovely
course nestled up against the foothills. They regularly host the
Hooper Tournament in June, the VFW Tournament in August and
the Trevino Tournament in September.

Ridgemark Golf & CC - Diablo

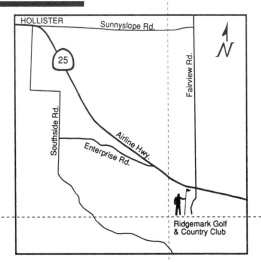

3800 Airline Highway
Hollister, CA 95023

(408) 637-1010

18 Hole Course

1991 Green Fees:

	Weekdays	Weekends
9 Holes:	n.a.	n.a.
18 Holes:	$20.00	$28.00
Twilight Rates:	$12.00	$15.00
Senior Discount: n.a.		

Equipment Rental:

Golf Cars - 9 Holes: Golf Cars - 18 Holes: $20.00
    Pull Carts: $2.00   Clubs: $20.00

Amenities:

Club Pro: Jim Crotz   Lessons: $25 / 30 Minutes
Ridgemark-Diablo offers Practice Putting and Chipping Greens and a
Driving Range. Bucket prices: $2.00 - $4.00. They have a Snack
Bar open from 6 a.m. until 5 p.m., plus a full restaurant and lounge
open from 5:30 until 9:30. The Pro Shop is complete. All reservations can be made seven days in advance beginning at 6:30 a.m.
This course is busiest on the weekends, least busy on Tuesdays.

Course Highlights:

The Ridgemark Golf & CC consists of 2, 18 hole, semi-private golf
courses. They alternate each day as to which course is open to the
public, keeping the other closed for members. The Diablo Course is
6,603 yards from the Blue Tees, 6,032 from the White Tees, and
5,427 from the Red Tees. Course ratings are: 72.4, 69.8 and 70.5,
respectively. Par for the course is 72. This course is nearly surrounded by homes nestled in the hills. The course is fairly tight,
generously sprinkled with water hazards. The greens you will find to
be huge, a plus for your approach shots. They host the new Frank
LaCorte Invitational.

San Benito County

87

Ridgemark Golf & CC - Gabilan

3800 Airline Highway
Hollister, CA 95023

(408) 637-1010

18 Hole Course

1991 Green Fees:

	Weekdays	Weekends
9 Holes:	n.a.	n.a.
18 Holes:	$20.00	$28.00
Twilight Rate:	$12.00	$15.00
Senior Discount:	n.a.	

Equipment Rental:

Golf Cars - 9 Holes:		Golf Cars - 18 Holes:	$20.00
Pull Carts:	$2.00	Clubs:	$20.00

Amenities:

Club Pro: Jim Cotz   Lessons: $25 / 30 Minutes
Ridgemark - Gabilan offers a Practice Putting and Chipping Green,
and a Driving Range. Bucket prices: $2.00 - $4.00. They have a
Snack Bar open from 6 a.m. until 5 p.m., plus a full restaurant and
lounge open from 5:30 until 9:30 p.m. The Pro Shop is complete.
Reservations can be made seven days in advance beginning at 6:30
a.m. This course is busiest on the weekends, least busy on Tuesdays.

Course Highlights:

The Ridgemark Golf & Country Club consists of 2, 18 hole, semi-
private golf courses. They alternate each day as to which course is
open to the public, keeping the other closed for members. The
Gabilan Course is 6,771 yards from the Blue Tees, 6,271 from the
White Tees, and 5,670 from the Red Tees. Course ratings are: 70.9,
68.6 and 70.8, respectively. Course Par is 72. This is a lovely,
scenic course, nestled in the hills. It is nearly surrounded by new
homes. In 1989 they introduced the Frank La Corte Invitational
Celebrity Baseball Tournament.

San Benito
County

88

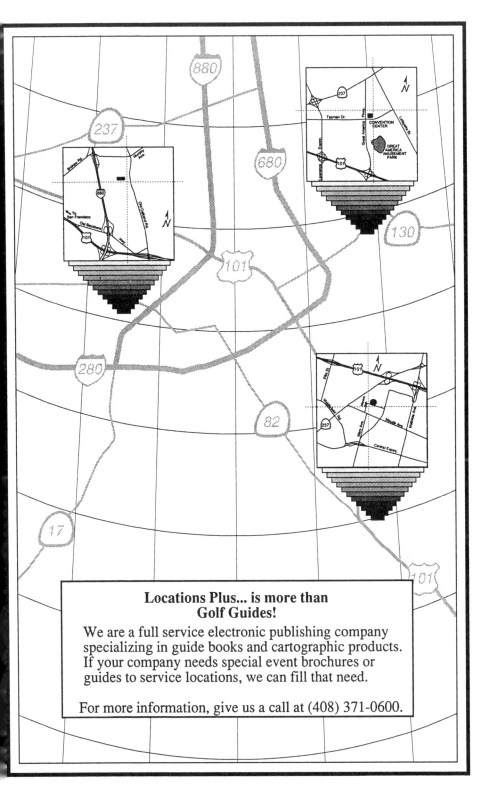

**Locations Plus... is more than
Golf Guides!**

We are a full service electronic publishing company
specializing in guide books and cartographic products.
If your company needs special event brochures or
guides to service locations, we can fill that need.

For more information, give us a call at (408) 371-0600.

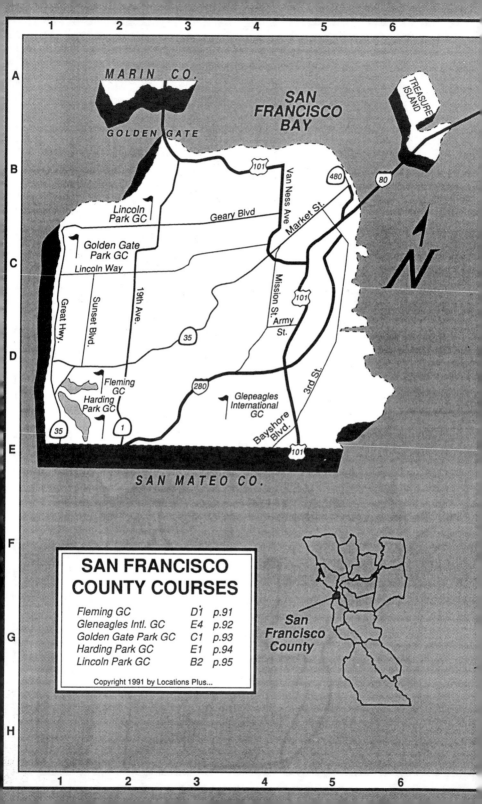

SAN FRANCISCO COUNTY COURSES

Fleming Golf Course

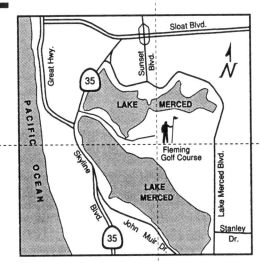

Harding Road at
   Skyline Blvd.
San Francisco, CA 94132

(415) 661-1865

9 Hole Course

1991 Green Fees

	Weekdays	Weekends
9 Holes:	$7.00	$8.00
18 Holes:	$14.00	$16.00
Twilight Rate:	$8.00	$10.00
Senior Discount:	Restricted to San Francisco residents	

Equipment Rental:

Golf Car - 9 Holes: Golf Car - 18 Holes: $18.00
   Pull Carts: $3.00   Clubs: $10.00

Amenities:

Club Pro: David Mutton   Lessons: $30 / 30 Minutes
Fleming Golf Course offers a Practice Putting Green and a Driving
Range. Bucket prices: $3 to $5. Their restaurant, "Benny's", is open
from 7 a.m. till dark, a lounge is also available. The Golf Shop is
complete. Weekday reservations can be made one working day in
advance. Weekend reservations can be made by SF City residents,
Tues. for Sat. and Wed. for Sun., beginning at 6:00 a.m.

Course Highlights:

This executive 9 hole course was designed by Jack Fleming nearly
60 years ago. Every hole is surrounded by lovely old pine trees. The
course is mostly flat except for a slight roll. There are 2,316 yards of
play to the course, par is 32. The holes consist of one par 5 hole at
460 yards long, three par 4 holes and the par 3 holes range from 150
to 220 yards long. The course is rated 31.3. Most golfers will be
pleased with the wide variety offered by this nine hole course.
Fleming Golf Course is part of the Harding Park Complex which
consists of 27 holes.

San Francisco County

91

Gleneagles International Golf Course

2100 Sunnydale Avenue
San Francisco, CA 94134

(415) 587-2425

9 Hole Course

1991 Green Fees

	Weekdays	Weekends
9 Holes:	$8.00	$10.00
18 Holes:	$13.00	$16.00

Twilight Rate: n.a.
Senior Discount: n.a.

Equipment Rental:

Golf Car - 9 Holes:	Golf Car - 18 Holes: $18.00
Pull Carts: n.a.	Clubs: n.a.

Amenities:

Club Pro: Mick Soli   Lessons: n.a.
There is a Practice Putting Green, but no Chipping Green or Driving Range available at Gleneagles. Their restaurant, "Old Peculiar's Public House", is open from dawn to dusk. A cocktail lounge is also available. Reservations only taken for weekends and holidays on the Monday prior, beginning at 7:00 a.m.

Course Highlights:

The course originally opened in 1962. It was rebuilt in 1980 and since then it has been rated one of the toughest 9 hole courses in California. It has a separate set of tees for playing a second nine holes. In 1985 The National Golf Foundation found this course to be among one of the 3 best 9 hole courses in the United States. The course was designed by Jack Fleming who also designed the Cypress Point Golf Course. Total yardage is 3,293, course par is 36. There are 2 par 5's, 2 par 3's and the rest are par 4's. Course rating is 71.1 and slope is 129.

Golden Gate Park Golf Course

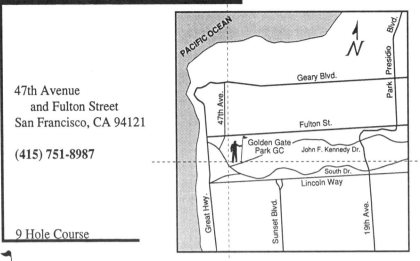

47th Avenue
    and Fulton Street
San Francisco, CA 94121

(415) 751-8987

9 Hole Course

1991 Green Fees	Weekdays	Weekends
9 Holes:	$5.00	$8.00
18 Holes:	$10.00	$16.00

Twilight Rate: n.a.
Senior Discount: Residents of San Francisco only.

Equipment Rental:

Golf Car - 9 Holes:	Golf Car - 18 Holes:	$8.00
Pull Carts: $3.50	Clubs: $6.	

Amenities:

Club Pro: Jim Ross   Lessons: Available
There is a Practice Putting Green available at Golden Gate Park Golf
Course, but no Chipping Green or Driving Range. Thiggy's Restaurant is open from 6 a.m. until sunset, daily, beer and wine are also
available. The Pro Shop will help in filling your golf needs. They do
not take reservations, first come, first serve. Fees subject to change
in June.

Course Highlights:

This is a 9 hole, par 3 golf course located in beautiful Golden Gate
Park. This is a convenient course allowing you the practice we all
need with our irons. Enjoy the relaxed atmosphere the Golden Gate
Park Golf Course offers.

San Francisco
County

Harding Park Golf Course

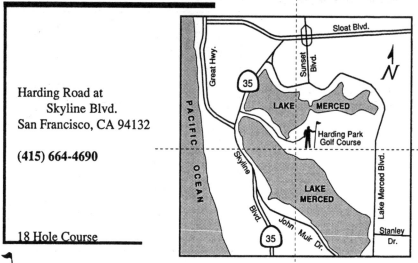

Harding Road at
   Skyline Blvd.
San Francisco, CA 94132

(415) 664-4690

18 Hole Course

1991 Green Fees	Weekdays	Weekends
9 Holes:	n.a.	n.a.
18 Holes:	$15.00	$20.00
Twilight Rate:	$8.00	$10.00

Senior Discount: Restricted to San Francisco residents

Equipment Rental:

Golf Car - 9 Holes:	Golf Car - 18 Holes: $18.00
Pull Carts: $3.00	Clubs: $10.00

Amenities:

Club Pro: David Mutton   Lessons: $30 / 30 Minutes
Harding Park Golf Course offers a Practice Putting Green and a
Driving Range. Bucket prices: $3 - $5. Their restaurant, "Benny's",
is open from 7 a.m. till dark, a lounge is also available. The Golf
Shop is complete. Weekday reservations can be made one working
day in advance. Weekend reservations can be made by SF City
residents, Tues. for Sat. and Wed. for Sun. at 6:00 a.m.

Course Highlights:

The course has been in operation since 1925. In 1963-1968 the
course played host to the Lucky Open on the PGA Tour and in 1981
the Eureka Senior Tour Event. This beautiful course, located in San
Francisco, has its boundaries set by a lake on 6 of its holes. This
course is long, 6,586 yards from the Men's Tees, Par 72, and 6,187
yards from the Women's Tees, Par 73. Fleming Golf Course, a nine
hole par 32 executive course, is part of this golf complex.

San Francisco
County

Lincoln Park Golf Course

34th Ave. and Clement St.
San Francisco, CA 94121

(415) 221-9911

18 Hole Course

1991 Green Fees

	Weekdays	Weekends
9 Holes:	n.a.	n.a.
18 Holes:	$13.00	$17.00
Twilight Rate:	$7.00	$9.00
Senior Discount:	San Francisco residents only	

Equipment Rental:

Golf Car - 9 Holes:	Golf Car - 18 Holes: $16.00
Pull Carts: $3.00	Clubs: $10.00

Amenities:

Club Pro: John Constantine   Lessons: $25 / 30 Minutes
Lincoln Park Golf Course offers a Practice Putting Green, but no
Chipping Green or Driving Range. Thiggy's Restaurant is open from
6:30 a.m. till 12:00 for you early diners. A cocktail lounge is also
available. Weekend reservations can be made three days in advance,
and one day in advance for weekdays. Fees subject to change in
June.

Course Highlights:

Lincoln Park Golf Course originally opened with just 6 holes, in
1916 it was expanded to include 18 holes. This golf course is
uniquely set around the Legion of Honor Art Museum, overlooking
the Pacific Ocean. From this vantage point, you will be able to enjoy
many splendid views of San Francisco while playing this lovely
course. Be sure to bring along a light jacket or windbreaker to ward
off any chilling winds swirling up from the Gate. The Men's course
rating is 65.3, the Women's is 68.2. Total yardage from the Men's
Tees is 5,149, Par 68. Total yardage from the Women's Tees is
4,984, Par 70.

San Francisco
County

95

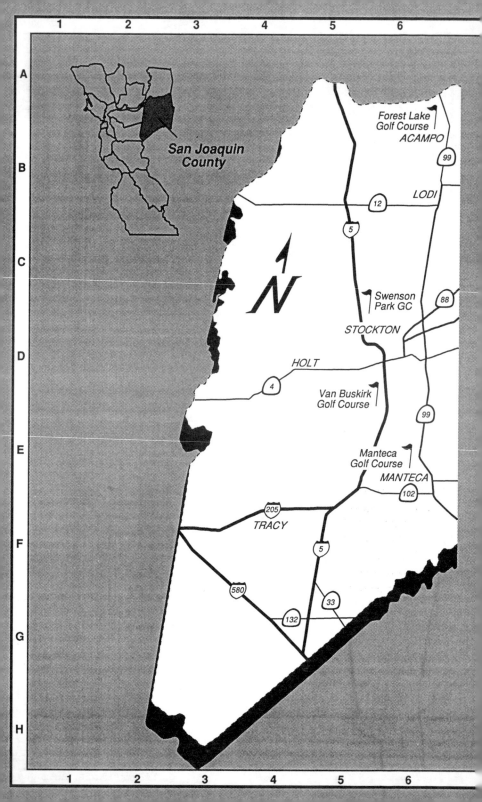

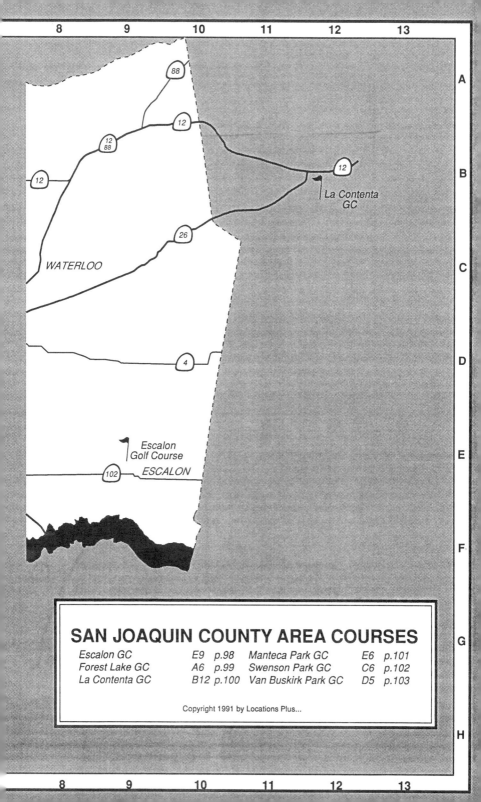

SAN JOAQUIN COUNTY AREA COURSES

Escalon GC	E9	p.98	Manteca Park GC	E6	p.101
Forest Lake GC	A6	p.99	Swenson Park GC	C6	p.102
La Contenta GC	B12	p.100	Van Buskirk Park GC	D5	p.103

Escalon Golf Course

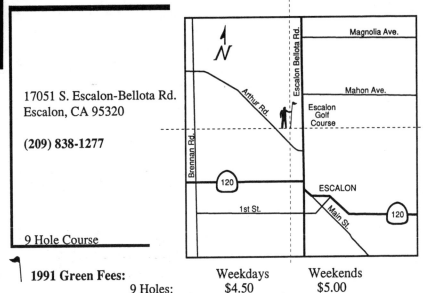

17051 S. Escalon-Bellota Rd.
Escalon, CA 95320

(209) 838-1277

9 Hole Course

1991 Green Fees:

	Weekdays	Weekends
9 Holes:	$4.50	$5.00
18 Holes:	$8.00	$9.00

Twilight Rate: n.a.
Senior Discount: n.a.

Equipment Rental:

Golf Cars - 9 Holes: n.a.   Golf Cars - 18 Holes: n.a.
   Pull Carts: $1.50   Clubs: $2.00

Amenities:

Club Pro: Tony Hall   Lessons: $25 / 60 Minutes
Escalon Golf Course offers a Practice Putting Green, Chipping Green
and a Driving Range. Bucket prices: $2.50 - $1.25. They provide a
Snack Bar which is open from 7 a.m. until dark, 7 days a week.
Reservations for Tee Times can be made at any time.

Course Highlights:

Escalon Golf Course originally opened as a driving range and two
years after that their 9 hole course was completed. It is a short 9
holes that plays for 1,520 yards. The longest hole is 250 yards, the
shortest is 70 yards. It is an intermediate course, not to be taken too
lightly. Escalon provides an enjoyable area for a walking round of
golf.

Forest Lake Golf Course

2450 Woodson Rd.
Acampo, CA 95220

(209) 369-5451

18 Hole Course

1991 Green Fees:

	Weekdays	Weekends
9 Holes:	$4.00	$7.00
18 Holes:	$6.00	$9.00

Twilight Rate: n.a.
Senior Discount: n.a.

Equipment Rental:

Golf Cars - 9 Holes: $7.00   Golf Cars - 18 Holes: $12.00
Pull Carts: $1.25   Clubs: $2.00

Amenities:

Club Pro: Brent Jensen   Lessons: $20 / 45 Minutes
Forest Lake Golf Course provides a Practice Putting Green, Chipping Green, Sand Trap and a Driving Range, bucket price is $1.00. Their Snack Bar and Pro Shop are open from dawn to dusk, daily. Reservations can be made one week in advance. Their least busy day of the week is Tuesday.

Course Highlights:

This is a lovely, well established, executive 18 hole course which has been in operation for the past 35 years. They have recently included additional holes that will vary the 18 holes in play. The course now measures 5,000 yards, and par for the course is 66. The many mature trees lining the fairways can become formidable obstacles if straight hitting is not yet a developed skill.

La Contenta Golf Club

1653 Highway 26
Valley Springs, CA 95252

(209) 772-1081

18 Hole Course

1991 Green Fees:

	Weekdays	Weekends
9 Holes:	n.a.	n.a.
18 Holes:	$15.00	$26.00
Twilight Rate:	$7.00	$13.00.

Senior Discount: $11.00 Monday - Thursday

Equipment Rental:

Golf Cars - 9 Holes: n.a.   Golf Cars - 18 Holes: $18.00
Pull Carts: $2.00   Clubs: $10.00

Amenities:

Club Pro: John Defilippi   Lessons: Yes

La Contenta Golf Club offers a practice area consisting of a netted hitting area, putting and chipping greens. Their newly expanded facility consisting of a clubhouse, restaurant and a pro shop that will more than meet the needs of the golfers. Reservations can be made two weeks in advance.

Course Highlights:

This is a 18 hole, semi-private course that provides a challenging game of golf, as well as an enjoyable outing. The course measures 6,500 yards and has a par of 72. It is a tight, rolling course bordered by homes on some of the holes, and sprinkled with streams and lakes on others. Their hole #13, which is a par 3, 175 yards is most memorable. The hole is quite scenic and often featured in Northern California golf articles.

100

Manteca Park Golf Course

305 N. Union Road
Manteca, CA 95336

(209) 823-5945

18 Hole Course

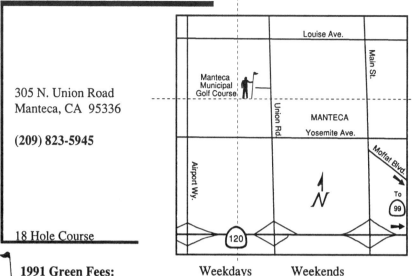

1991 Green Fees:	Weekdays	Weekends
9 Holes:	$7.00	$8.00
18 Holes:	$10.75	$14.25

Twilight Rate: $7.00
Senior Discount: $3.00 after 11:00 p.m. on Tuesdays only.

Equipment Rental:

Golf Cars - 9 Holes: $10.00   Golf Cars - 18 Holes: $18.00
    Pull Carts: $2.00   Clubs: $8.00

Amenities:

Club Pro: Alan Thomas   Lessons: $25.00
There is a Practice Putting Green and a Driving Range available
Bucket prices: $2.50 - $4.00. Their Snack Bar is open from 7 a.m.
until 7 p.m. for you convenience. The Pro Shop's inventory is
extensive. Reservations can be made 7 days in advance for weekdays and the Monday prior for the weekend. This 18 hole course is
busiest on Saturdays.

Course Highlights:

Manteca Park Golf Course opened in 1966 with 9 holes and in 1978
added an additional 9. The fairways are narrow, the rough is thick
and there are lateral water hazards on seven of the holes. Yardages
range from 6,447 from the Championship Tees, 6,281 from the
Regular Tees and 5,739 from the Ladies' Tees. The course is rated
70.2, 69.2 and 72.1, respectively. Par is 72. Their new clubhouse,
pro shop and restaurant should be completed by June of 1991.

101

Swenson Park Golf Course

6803 Alexandria Pl.
Stockton, CA 95212

(209) 477-0774

27 Hole Course

1991 Green Fees:

	Weekdays	Weekends
9 Holes:	$4.75	$5.25
18 Holes:	$8.00	$9.00

Twilight Rate: $1.00 off
Senior Discount: $4.50 after 11:00 - with monthly card

Equipment Rental:

Golf Cars - 9 Holes: $9.00   Golf Cars - 18 Holes: $16.00
Pull Carts: $1.50   Clubs: $7.00

Amenities:

Club Pro: Ernie George   Lessons: $25 / 45 Minutes
There is a Practice Putting Green, Chipping Green and a Driving
Range at Swenson Park. Bucket Prices: $1.50 - $3.00. Their Snack
Bar is open from 6 a.m. until 6 p.m. daily. Their Pro Shop is
complete. Weekend reservations can be made early on the Monday
prior, for weekdays, 7 days in advance. They are busiest on the
weekends, least busy on Mondays and Tuesdays.

Course Highlights:

Swenson Park has been in operation since 1950. They have an
executive 9 hole course as well as a regulation 18 hole. There are
plenty of trees on the course and you will find a lot of elevated
greens. The 9 hole course is a par 3 and plays for 1,380 yards. The
18 hole course is rated 69.1, slope is 110. Total yards from the Men's
Tees is 6,407, par is 72. From the Women's Tees it is 6,266 and par
is 74.

102

Van Buskirk Park Golf Course

1740 Houston Ave.
Stockton, CA 95206

(209) 464-5629

18 Hole Course

1991 Green Fees:

	Weekdays	Weekends
9 Holes:	n.a.	n.a.
18 Holes:	$8.00	$9.00

Twilight Rate: $7.00
Senior Discount: $5.50 after 11:00 p.m.

Equipment Rental:

Golf Cars - 9 Holes:	Golf Cars - 18 Holes: $16.00
Pull Carts: $2.00	Clubs: $3.00

Amenities:

Club Pro: Jose Santiago   Lessons: $20 / 30 Minutes
There is a Practice Putting Green and a Driving Range available at
Van Buskirk Golf Course. A bucket of balls is $2.00. Their Snack
Bar is open from 6 a.m. until 6 p.m. There is also a Pro Shop to fill
your immediate golfing needs. Golf reservations can be made one
week in advance for weekdays, and on the Monday prior for the
weekend.

Course Highlights:

This 18 hole course is owned by the City of Stockton Department of
Parks & Recreation. It runs along the San Joaquin River which adds
to the pleasantness of the course. It plays fairly long with 6,572
yards from the Men's Tees and 6,200 from the Ladies'. It is rated
69.3, par 72 for the Men and 73.5, par 74, slope 114 for the Ladies.

103

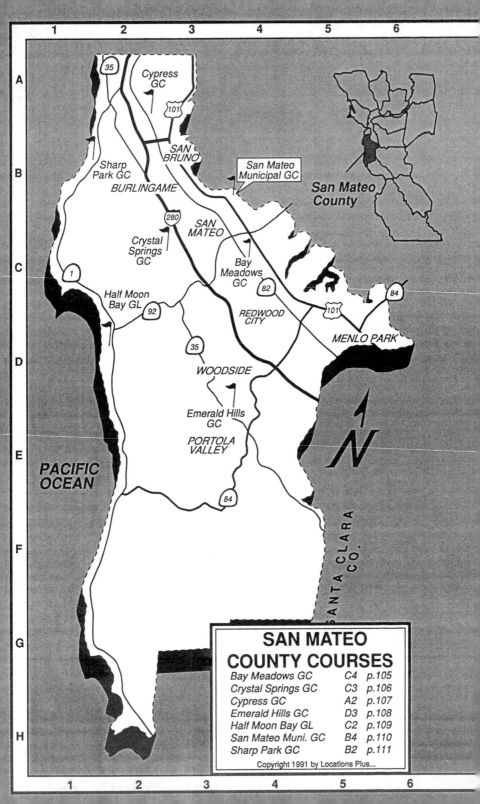

SAN MATEO
COUNTY COURSES

Bay Meadows Golf Course

2600 South Delaware Street
San Mateo, CA 94402

(415) 341-7204

9 Hole Course

1991 Green Fees:

	Weekdays	Weekends
9 Holes:	$5.00	$5.00
18 Holes:		

Twilight Rate: n.a
Senior Discount: 10 Play Card for $40.00

Equipment Rental:

Golf Car - 9 Holes:	n.a.	Golf Car - 18 Holes:	n.a.
Pull Carts:	$2.00	Clubs:	$3.00

Amenities:

Club Pro: n.a.   Lessons: n.a.

This course is open 7 days a week from the end of January through the beginning of August. The remainder of the time, when the races are being held at Bay Meadows, they are only open Monday and Tuesday. They do have a Snack Bar for your convenience. They do not take reservations, first come, first serve.

Course Highlights:

This nine hole, par three course sits in the middle of the Bay Meadows Race Track. At first, it was just a driving range till about 15 years ago when they turned it into a Par 3 course. Total yardage is 1,365 and par is 28. There are 8 par 3 holes and 1 par 4. The course is flat and easy to walk, ideal for beginners and seniors. There are 250 to 300 golfers a day out here at Bay Meadows during the months of May, June and July.

Crystal Springs Golf Club

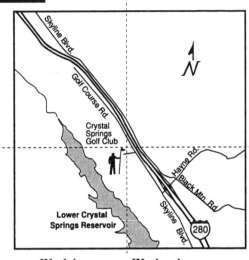

6650 Golf Course Drive
Burlingame, CA 94010

(415) 342-0603

18 Hole Course

1991 Green Fees:

	Weekdays	Weekends
9 Holes:	n.a.	n.a.
18 Holes:	$35.00	$40.00
Twilight Rate: After 2:30	$28.00	$34.00
Senior Discount: n.a.		

Equipment Rental:

Golf Car - 9 Holes: $16.00   Golf Car - 18 Holes: $22.00
Pull Carts: $3.00   Clubs: $15.00 + tax

Amenities:

Club Pro: Roger Graves   Lessons: $30 / 30 Minutes
A Putting Green and Driving Range are available, but no Chipping
Green. Bucket prices: $2.00 - $4.00. Their restaurant is open from
8 a.m. until 6 p.m., a cocktail lounge is also available. The Pro
Shop carries a full line of golf accessories. Weekend reservations
can be made on the prior Monday after 6:00 a.m. and for weekdays,
seven days in advance. Least busy day is Monday.

Course Highlights:

This course, designed by W. Herbert Fowler, opened in 1924.
It was later redesigned by Billy Bell, Jr. Course yardages and ratings
are: Championship 6,683, 71.1, Regular 6,321, 69.9, and Ladies'
5,890, 71.2. Par for the course is 72. The course record of 63 is held
by Charles Leider. As you make your way around this beautiful
course, you may run across an unexpected critter. Located on a
watershed, this course draws an abundance of wildlife, perhaps one
or two Bobcats will make an appearance at your golf outing.

Cypress Golf Course

2001 Hillside Blvd.
Colma, CA 94014

(415) 992-5155

9 Hole Course

1991 Green Fees:

	Weekdays	Weekends
9 Holes:	$10.00	$15.00
18 Holes:		

Twilight Rate: n.a.

Senior Discount: $5.00 before 9:00 a.m. Monday-Friday

Equipment Rental:

Golf Car - 9 Holes: $10.00   Golf Car - 18 Holes: $20.00
          Pull Carts: $2.00   Clubs: n.a.

Amenities:

Club Pro: Don Giovannini   Lessons: $30 / 60 Minutes
Cypress Golf Course offers a Practice Putting Green, Chipping Green and a Driving Range. Bucket prices: $4.00 - $6.00. Licata's restaurant, lounge is available. The Pro Shop carries a limited inventory of golf equipment. Reservations can be made one week in advance. Their least busy days are Mondays and Tuesdays.

Course Highlights:

Cypress Golf Course, formerly known as Cypress Hills, was developed in the early 1960's. It was originally a 9 hole, par 3 course, was changed to include 18 holes, and now is once again a 9 hole course. It boasts of being one of the longest 9 hole courses in California measuring 3,443 yards. There is only one par 3 hole, two par 5 holes and the rest are par 4's. The longest par 5 is 530 yards long. Par for the course is 37, course record is 33. The course is somewhat hilly, the fairways are tree lined and you will encounter water on 2 of the holes. This is a difficult, but fun to play, course.

107

Emerald Hills Golf Course

1059 Wilmington Way
Redwood City, CA 94062

(415) 368-7820

9 Hole Course

1991 Green Fees:

	Weekdays	Weekends
9 Holes:	$6.00	$7.00
18 Holes:	$10.00	$12.00

Twilight Rate: n.a.
Senior Discount: $3.00 for 9 Holes during the week

Equipment Rental:

Golf Car - 9 Holes:	n.a.	Golf Car - 18 Holes:	
Pull Carts:	n.a.	Clubs:	$3.00

Amenities:

Club Pro: n.a.   Lessons: n.a.

There is a Practice Putting Green and a Chipping Green available at Emerald Hills Golf Course. In the Pro Shop you will find assorted beverages and snacks along with a limited supply of golf accessories. They do not take reservations.

Course Highlights:

Emerald Hills Golf Course belongs to the Elk's Lodge, but is still open to the public. The course is short measuring 1,163 yards from the Men's Tees and 1,138 yards from the Ladies' Tees. Emerald Hills is well named for its location. This course will present a challenge to most golfers because of its many trees and narrow fairways. Bring along a fishing pole, if the golf is not going well, try your luck in one of the three ponds you will find on the course.

108

Half Moon Bay Golf Links

2000 Fairway Drive
Half Moon Bay, CA 94019

(415) 726-4438

18 Hole Course

1991 Green Fees: | Weekdays | Weekends
| 9 Holes: | n.a. | n.a.
| 18 Holes: | $60.00 | $80.00
| Twilight Rate: After 2 / 3 p.m. | $40.00 | $45.00 Sunday
| Senior Discount: n.a.

Equipment Rental: Golf Car included in Green Fee
Golf Car - 9 Holes: Golf Car - 18 Holes:
    Pull Carts: n.a.   Clubs: $15.00

Amenities:

Club Pro: Moon Mullins   Lessons: $30 / 30 Minutes
A Practice Putting Green and Chipping Green are available at Half
Moon Bay Golf Links, but no Driving Range. Enterprize Saloon
Restaurant and Lounge is open from 7 a.m. until 8 p.m. for your
convenience. Their Pro Shop carries a full line of golf accessories.
Reservations can be made 7 days in advance, Sat. for Sat., etc.,
beginning at day break. They offer a replay for $20.00

Course Highlights:

Half Moon Bay Golf Links opened in October of 1973. Designer of
the course is Francis Duane with Arnold Palmer as a consultant.
Remodeling of the restaurant, lounge and Pro Shop was completed in
1989. The greens and fairways have been overhauled adding to the
playability of the course. The course rating is 74.5. Total yardage
from the Championship Tees is 7,116. The Johnny Walker Red
Label Rock and Roll Golf Tournament is held here annually. This
challenging course has more then its fair share of hazards, including
barrancas.

San Mateo Municipal Golf Course

Coyote Point Drive
San Mateo, CA 94401

(415) 347-1461

18 Hole Course

1991 Green Fees:

	Weekdays	Weekends
9 Holes:	n.a.	n.a.
18 Holes:	$9.50	$11.50

Twilight Rate: 9 Holes $8.00 after 3:00 p.m.
Senior Discount: $7.00 - San Mateo residents

Equipment Rental:

Golf Car - 9 Holes:	Golf Car - 18 Holes:	$16.00
Pull Carts: $2.00	Clubs: $8.00	

Amenities:

Club Pro: Jake Montes   Lessons: $17.50 / 30 Minutes
There is a Practice Putting Green and a Chipping Green at San Mateo
Golf Course. The First Tee Restaurant is open from 6 a.m. until 4:00
daily. There is a separate cocktail lounge. The Pro Shop will be able
to fill your golfing needs. Reservations can be made seven days in
advance. Their busiest days of the week are Wednesdays through
Sundays, the least busy day is Monday.

Course Highlights:

This 18 hole course sits out on Coyote Point, subject to all the
breezes of the Bay. The course is flat with narrow fairways. There
is a reservoir on hole #6, and a creek runs along holes #3, 14, 16 and
#17. There is a lake on hole #18. The course from the Blue Tees is
5,853 yards and is rated 66.5, from the White Tees it is 5,496 yards
and is rated 64.7 and from the Gold it is 5,451 yards and is rated
69.7. Par 70 / 72.

110

Sharp Park Golf Course

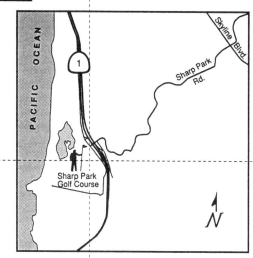

Highway 1
Pacifica, CA 94044

(415) 359-3380

18 Hole Course

1991 Green Fees:

	Weekdays	Weekends
9 Holes:	$7.00	$9.00
18 Holes:	$13.00	$17.00
Twilight Rate:	$7.00	$9.00

Senior Discount: $7 Wdkys. / $12 Wknds. with resident cards.

Equipment Rental:

Golf Car - 9 Holes: $10.00		Golf Car - 18 Holes: $18.00
Pull Carts: $3.00		Clubs: $5.00

Amenities:

Club Pro: Jack R. Gage   Lessons: $25 / 30 Minutes
Sharp Park offers a Practice Putting Green and a Chipping Green.
They have a full restaurant serving from 6 a.m. until 10 p.m. The Pro
Shop carries a complete line of golf equipment. Reservations for
Saturday Tee Times can be made on Wednesdays prior, and for
Sunday Tee Times on Thursdays prior. Weekday reservations can be
made on Sundays.

Course Highlights:

This 18 hole links course is often referred to as "The Poor Man's
Pebble Beach". The back 9 holes run along the shore of the Pacific
Ocean providing the golfer with beautiful views as well as an
occasional stiff ocean breeze. The course is heavily treed, has
several water holes and the greens are fairly small. The course was
designed by Alister Mackenzie, and built by Jack Fleming in 1929.
The course plays for a total of 6,273 yards and is rated 70.0 from the
Men's Tees, slope 115. The Ladies' rating is 73.0 and slope is 120.
Par for the course is 72, course record is 63 and held by George
Archer.

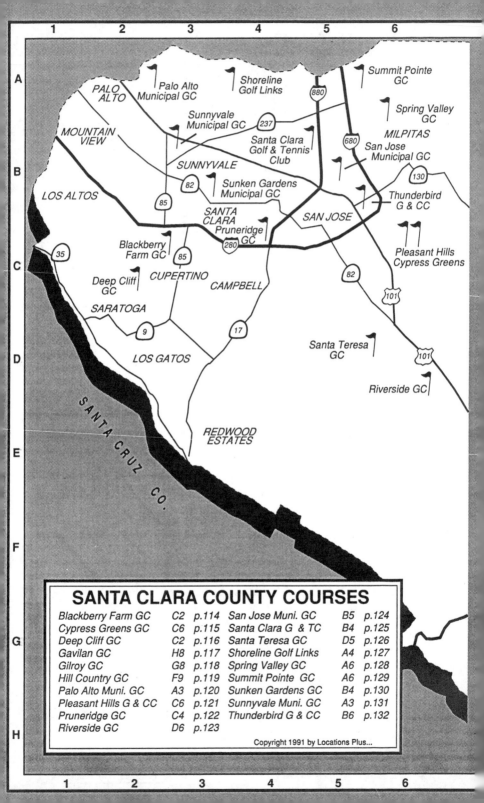

SANTA CLARA COUNTY COURSES

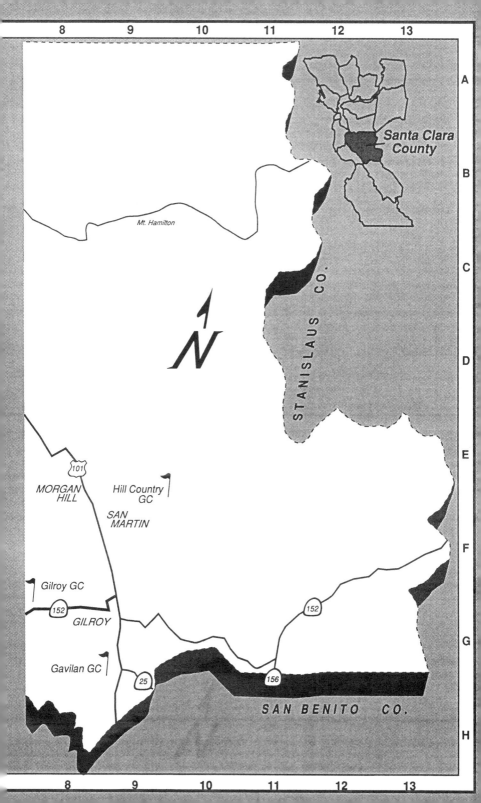

Blackberry Farm Golf Course

22100 Stevens Creek Blvd.
Cupertino, CA 95014

(408) 253-9200

9 Hole Course

1991 Green Fees:

	Weekdays	Weekends
9 Holes:	$5.75	$7.50
18 Holes:	$10.50	$13.00

Twilight Rate: n.a.
Senior Discount: $1.00 less on weekdays only.

Equipment Rental:

Golf Cars - 9 Holes:	n.a.	Golf Cars - 18 Holes:	n.a.
Pull Carts:	$2.00	Clubs:	$4.50

Amenities:

Club Pro: Jeff Piserchio   Lessons: $28/ 40 Minutes
There is a Practice Putting Green, a netted hitting enclosure but no
Chipping Green. The Blue Pheasant Restaurant serves both lunch
and dinner, cocktails are available in the lounge. Their Pro Shop is
small, but can fill all your golfing needs. All reservations can be
made one week in advance beginning early a.m.

Course Highlights:

This course is a short par 29 at 1,625 yards. The longest hole, #2,
is 292 yards followed by hole #4 at 278 yards; all other holes fall
below the 200 yard mark. The 6th hole is the shortest at 101 yards.
Water will come into play on four of the holes, a substantial water
hazard must be negotiated from the tee box on the 8th hole. A
wise club selection is needed on the 3rd hole since it plays shorter
due to the tee's elevation, the ball can easily clear the surrounding
fence or ricochet off a nearby maintenance building. A high fence
and a deep creek bed will shadow the 7th, 8th and 9th holes and
may cause some golfers to over-compensate. This is a narrow
course so any combination of hooks or slices can lead to a frustrat-
ing day of golf.

114

Cypress Greens Golf Course

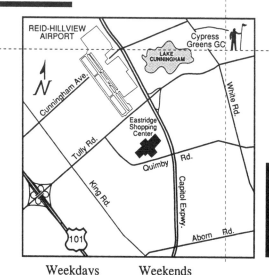

2050 South White Road
San Jose, CA 95151

(408) 238-3485

18 Hole Course

1991 Green Fees:

	Weekdays	Weekends
9 Holes:	n.a.	n.a.
18 Holes:	$6.00	$8.00

Twilight Rate: n.a.
Senior Discount: Yes

Equipment Rental:

Golf Cars - 9 Holes:	Golf Cars - 18 Holes: n.a.
Pull Carts: $2.50	Clubs: $10.00

Amenities:

Club Pro: n.a.   Lessons: n.a.

There is a Practice Putting Green and a Chipping Green but no Driving Range here at Cypress Greens. The restaurant and lounge are open daily for your convenience. The Pro Shop will help fill your immediate golfing needs. Reservations are not necessary, first come, first serve.

Course Highlights:

Cypress Greens is an eighteen hole, par 3 golf course. It is predominantly a straight course with the exception of a severe dogleg on the 17th hole. Mature trees line most of the fairways, and a lake will come into play on three of the holes providing we get more rain than last year. This course measures 2,631 yards long. Par for the course is 54. To get away from the crowds and enjoy a short game of golf try Cypress Greens.

Deep Cliff Golf Course

10700 Clubhouse Lane
Cupertino, CA 95014

(408) 253-5357

18 Hole Course

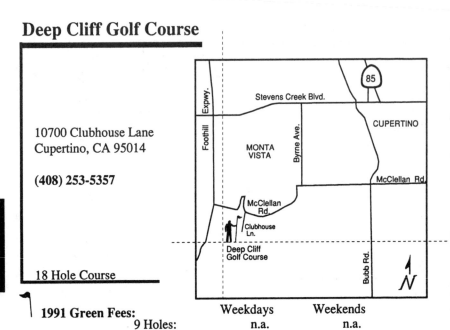

1991 Green Fees:

	Weekdays	Weekends
9 Holes:	n.a.	n.a.
18 Holes:	$13.00	17.00
Twilight Rate:	$10.00	$13.00
Senior Discount: n.a.		

Equipment Rental:

Golf Cars - 9 Holes: n.a.   Golf Cars - 18 Holes: n.a.
      Pull Carts: $2.00   Clubs: $3.00 - $7.00

Amenities:

Club Pro: Scott Cline   Lessons: n.a.
There is a Practice Putting Green but no Driving Range at Deep
Cliff Golf Course. The Snack Bar remains open from 8 a.m. until
dusk. Reservations can be made six days in advance by phone,
otherwise, seven days in advance.

Course Highlights:

The front nine holes were constructed in 1961 and the back nine in
1962. During 1989 many improvements were made to the course
including rebuilding of the Tees and Greens. There are numerous
elevated tees and rolling fairways. Tall Pine trees and a wandering
creek will come into play on more than half of the holes. This is a
relatively short course at 3,654 yards from the Men's Tees and
3,424 from the Women's. The course par is a modest 60. The
longest hole is the 2nd at 327 yards, a par 4. The 17th hole is the
shortest at 100 yards. Par 3's range from 100 to 186 yards. This is
a course that will reward the finesse golfer.

Gavilan Golf Course

5055 Santa Teresa Blvd.
Gilroy, GC 95020

(408) 848-1363

9 Hole Course

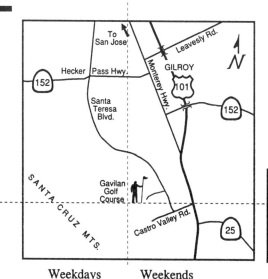

1991 Green Fees:

	Weekdays	Weekends
9 Holes:	$8.00	$10.00
18 Holes:	$8.00	$10.00
Twilight Rate: After 3 / 4 p.m.	$5.00	$5.00
Senior Discount: $6.00 Weekdays only		

Equipment Rental:

Golf Cars - 9 Holes: $10.00   Golf Cars - 18 Holes: $10.00
    Pull Carts: $1.00   Clubs: $2.00

Amenities:

Club Pro: None   Lessons: n.a.
Gavilan Golf Course offers a Practice Putting Green, Chipping
Green and a Driving Range. Bucket prices: $1.00 - $3.00. This is
a nine hole course with the tees offset to change the distances and
angles for the back nine. Snacks and beverages are available along
with a number of golf accessories at the Pro Shop. They do not
take reservations.

Course Highlights:

The course opened in 1968 and abuts Gavilan College. This is a
short course at only 3,638 yards from both the Men's and Women's
Tees. Pars are 62 for the men and 63 for the women. Although the
course is short the distance seems greater if you're walking due to
the rolling terrain. This is especially true on the #2 and #9 holes.
An out-of-bounds fence and roadway shadows the 3rd hole on the
right side. Water comes into play only on the 8th hole, a decep-
tively short par 3, 87 yards. The holes will range in length from
the 8th at 87 yards to the 3rd at 356 yards.

Gilroy Golf Course

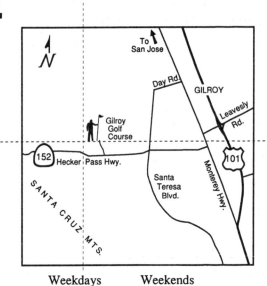

2695 Hecker Pass Hwy.
Gilroy, CA 95020

(408) 842-2501

18 Hole Course

1991 Green Fees:

	Weekdays	Weekends
9 Holes:	$10.00	$16.00
18 Holes:	$10.00	$16.00
Twilight Rate:	$8.00	$10.00

Senior Discount: 25%

Equipment Rental:

Golf Cars - 9 Holes: $10.00   Golf Cars - 18 Holes: $18.00
Pull Carts: $2.00   Clubs: $6.00

Amenities:

Club Pro: Don DeLorenzo   Lessons: $20 / 30 Minutes
A Driving Range, Chipping Green and Practice Putting Green are
available at Gilroy. The Gilroy Golf Course Restaurant is open
from 10 a.m. until 3 p.m. The Pro Shop carries a full line of golf
equipment. Reservations can be made seven days in advance.
Their busiest day of the week is Friday, least busy on Thursday.

Course Highlights:

The course was opened in the early 1920's and hosts the "Gilroy
Garlic Festival Golf Tournament" and the "Special Olympics
Tournament". This course will play longer than the 5,798 yards
from the Men's Tees or 5,501 from the Women's, due to a number
of fairways hugging the hillsides. The course record of 61 is held
by George Archer. Par from the Men's Tees is 70 while the
Women's Par is 72. The holes will range in length from a 511
yard, par 5 on #4 to 130 yard, par 3 on the 14th. There are areas on
this course where you will be hitting the ball from a blind spot.
You need to be a good judge of distance to score well on these
tough holes.

Hill Country Golf Course

15060 Foothill Avenue
Morgan Hill, CA 95037

(408) 779-4136

18 Hole Course

1991 Green Fees:

	Weekdays	Weekends
9 Holes:	n.a.	n.a.
18 Holes:	$7.00	$10.00

Twilight Rate: n.a.
Senior Discount: $5.00 Tuesdays & Thursdays

Equipment Rental:

Golf Cars - 9 Holes:	Golf Cars - 18 Holes: $10.00
Pull Carts: $2.00	Clubs: n.a.

Amenities:

Club Pro: Jan Perch   Lessons: *$25 / 30 Minutes
Hill Country Golf Course is closed on Mondays. Their warm-up
facility is a Practice Putting Green. The Flying Lady Restaurant is
open from 12:00 noon to 2:30 p.m. and 5:00 p.m. to 8:30 p.m. on
Wed. thru Sun; closed on Mon. and Tues. Cocktails are available
in the lounge. There is a Pro Shop for your convenience. Reservations can be made at anytime. *George Ekberg is the teaching pro.

Course Highlights:

The course opened in 1974. During the last half of 1988 a great
deal of improvements were made, most notably the rebuilding of
the greens. If you enjoy the challenge of water hazards you will
enjoy this course. On ten of the holes water comes into play, on
six of the holes you will need to traverse water to approach the
greens. This is a short, par 58, course. From the Men's Tees the
distance is 3,110 yards and from the Women's only 2,753 yards.
There are four par 4 holes and the remaining are par 3's. The
longest hole is #1, par 4, at 368 yards, with the 7th hole being the
shortest at 98 yards. This course offers an abundance of work for
those short irons.

Palo Alto Municipal Golf Course

1875 Embarcadero Road
Palo Alto, CA 94303

(415) 856-0881

18 Hole Course

1991 Green Fees:

	Weekdays	Weekends
9 Holes:	*$8.00	*$9.00
18 Holes:	$13.00	$17.00
Twilight Rate:	$8.00	$11.00

Senior Discount: Palo Alto residents only.

Equipment Rental:

Golf Cars - 9 Holes:	Golf Cars - 18 Holes: $17.00
Pull Carts: $3.00	Clubs: $12.50

Amenities:

Club Pro: Brad Lozares   Lessons: $25 / 30 Minutes
This course offers a Practice Putting Green and a Driving Range.
Bucket prices: $2.25 - $4.50. Harry's Hofbrau is open 7 a.m. to 6
p.m. Brad Lozares' Golf Shop is complete. Weekend reservations
can be made on the Tuesday prior beginning at 7:00 a.m. and 7
days in advance for weekdays. They are least busy Mon. thru
Thur. after 1:00. *9 Hole Fees apply the 1st 1/2 hour from back 9.

Course Highlights:

The course opened in 1956 and has been redesigned by Robert
Trent Jones, Jr. The course is a long par 72 for the men and 73 for
the women. Yardage from the Men's Tees is 6,525 and from the
Women's 5,852 yards. If you are playing from the Pro Tees the
distance is 6,854 yards. This is a relatively straight course, with
only one water hazard. The holes will range from a long 521
yards, par 5, on #1 to a short 149 yards, par 3, on #3. The course
record of 64 is held by Brad Heninger. The course hosts numerous
tournaments including the Times Tribune Jr. Championship , The
Palo Alto Senior Men's and Women's Championships, Santa Clara
Valley Best Ball and the Towne & Country Women's Championship.

120

Pleasant Hills Golf & Country Club

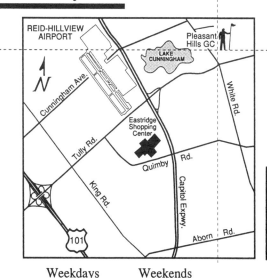

2050 South White Road
San Jose, CA 95151

(408) 238-3485

18 Hole Course

1991 Green Fees:

	Weekdays	Weekends
9 Holes:	n.a.	n.a.
18 Holes:	$16.00	$20.00
Twilight Rate: After 3:00 p.m	$10.00	$12.00
Senior Discount: $10.00 all day, weekdays only		

Equipment Rental:

Golf Cars - 9 Holes:	Golf Cars - 18 Holes: $16.00
Pull Carts: $2.50	Clubs: $10.00

Amenities:

Club Pro: n.a.   Lessons: n.a.

Pleasant Hills Golf & Country Club offers a Practice Putting Green and a Chipping Green, but no Driving Range. Their clubhouse serves a variety of food and beverages. The Pro Shop carries a limited amount of golf equipment. Reservations can be made one week in advance.

Course Highlights:

Pleasant Hills Golf and Country Club is 30 years old. No major renovations in the last several years. The course is one of two at the same location and set back far enough from the major roads to give a feeling of seclusion. The course is relatively flat with gentle rolling fairways. The fairways are wide but are lined with numerous mature trees. This is a long course measuring 6,888 yards from the Blue Tees, 6,519 from the White Tees, and 6,084 from the Red Tees. Par for the Men is 72; Women's par is 75.

121

Pruneridge Golf Course

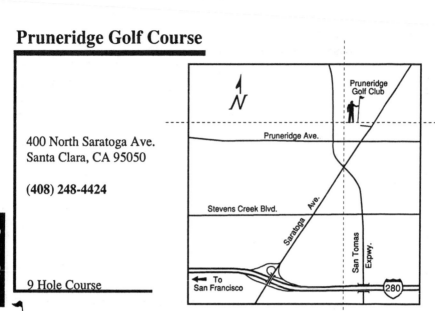

400 North Saratoga Ave.
Santa Clara, CA 95050

(408) 248-4424

9 Hole Course

1991 Green Fees:

	Weekdays	Weekends
9 Holes:	$6.50	$7.50
18 Holes:	$13.00	$15.00

Twilight Rate: n.a.
Senior Discount: With membership fee of $10.00

Equipment Rental:

Golf Cars - 9 Holes: n.a.	Golf Cars - 18 Holes: n.a.
Pull Carts: $1.50	Clubs: $5.00

Amenities:

Club Pro: Kevin MacKay   Lessons: $30 / 45 Minutes
A Practice Putting Green and Driving Range are available at
Pruneridge. Bucket prices range from $2.00 - $6.00. The Pro
Shop carries a large selection of golf accessories. There is also a
Snack Bar open from dawn to dusk featuring deli-type sandwiches
and beverages. Reservations are taken one week in advance
beginning at daybreak.

Course Highlights:

The course was built on the site of a former prune orchard in 1964
by Charlie & Betty Lester Boyd. At that time the course was
known as "Pruneridge Farms Golf Course". The course was sold
in 1977 and the new owner changed the name to "Pruneridge Golf
Club". Remodeling of the course was completed in 1978 with the
help of Robert Trent Jones, Jr. This nine hole course is 1,959
yards in length and includes five par 3's and four par 4's. The
course has an NCGA rating of 56.6. Golf memberships are
available, if interested contact the club for details.

Riverside Golf Course

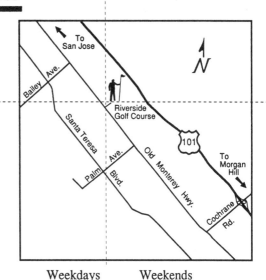

Old Monterey Highway
Coyote, CA 95013

(408) 463-0622

18 Hole Course

1991 Green Fees:

	Weekdays	Weekends
9 Holes:	n.a.	n.a.
18 Holes:	$17.00	$22.00
Twilight Rate:	$13.00	$17.00

Senior Discount: $13.00 wkdys. with purchase of Senior card

Equipment Rental:

Golf Cars - 9 Holes: n.a.   Golf Cars - 18 Holes: $21.00
     Pull Carts: $5.00   Clubs: $10.00

Amenities:

Club Pro: Tom Smith   Lessons: $30 / 30 Minutes
A Practice Putting Green and a Driving Range are available at
Riverside. The Pro Shop carries a full line of merchandise for
your golfing needs. The Riverside Restaurant is open from 8 a.m.
until 4 p.m. serving snacks and beverages. Reservations can be
made starting at 12:00 noon on Saturday for the following Saturday & Sunday and one week in advance for weekdays.

Course Highlights:

The course opened in 1957. The course is rated 71 from the
Championship Tees and 69 from the Regular Tees. 6,825 yards
and 6,504 yards respectively, Par 72. The official course record is
a 67 with an unsanctioned course record of 63. The course hosts a
number of tournaments each year which include the "American
Cancer Society" and "The Mark Winters Leukemia Memorial".
The course is south of San Jose and situated between Highway 101
on the east and Old Monterey Highway on the west. The entrance
is from Old Monterey Highway between Palm and Bailey Av-
enues.

San Jose Municipal Golf Course

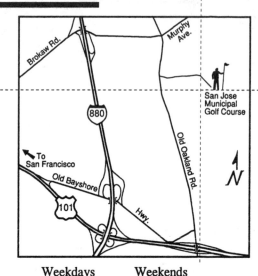

1560 Old Oakland Road
San Jose, CA 95131

(408) 441-4653

Santa Clara County

18 Hole Course

1991 Green Fees:

	Weekdays	Weekends
9 Holes:	*$12.00	*$15.00
18 Holes:	$18.00	$25.00
Twilight Rate: After 2 / 3 p.m.	$12.00	$15.00

Senior Discount: $12.00 on weekdays with San Jose resident card

Equipment Rental:

Golf Cars - 9 Holes: $11.00	Golf Cars - 18 Holes: $20.00
Pull Carts: $2..50	Clubs: $10.00

Amenities:

Club Pro: Mike Rawitser   Lessons: Yes
San Jose Municipal has a Practice Putting Green, Chipping Green
and a Driving Range. Bucket prices: $2.00 - $5.00. A Pro Shop,
Restaurant and Cocktail Lounge will fill most golfers' require-
ments. Weekend reservations taken on the prior Tuesday at 7:00
a.m. and one week in advance for weekdays. *The first hour of the
day from back 9.

Course Highlights:

The course opened in 1968. This is a long course at 6,401 yards
from the Men's Tees, 5,484 yards from the Women's Tees and
6,916 from the Pro's Tees. The 11th hole, par 5, is 530 yards and
is the longest on the course. Bunkers will come into play on nearly
every hole, most commonly near the greens. The length on some
of the par 3's will pose difficulty in club selection. For example,
the 17th hole is a par 3 at 170 yards and a difficult play over water
with two traps skirting the green. The proper club selection will
make a tremendous difference on this hole. San Jose Municipal
also serves as home to a number of Prairie Owls, it can make
searching for that hooked ball an interesting wildlife outing.

Santa Clara Golf & Tennis Club

5155 Stars and Stripes Dr.
Santa Clara, CA 95054

(408) 980-9515

18 Hole Course

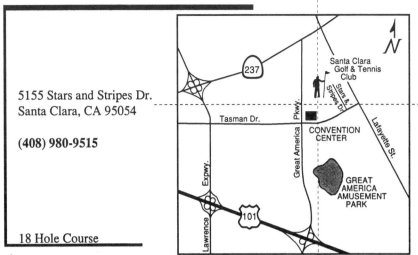

1991 Green Fees:

	Weekdays	Weekends
9 Holes:	n.a.	n.a.
18 Holes:	$14.00	$20.00
Twilight Rate:	$8.00	$12.00

Senior Discount: $60.00 per month weekdays only

Equipment Rental:

Golf Cars - 9 Holes: $8.00   Golf Cars - 18 Holes: $16.00
Pull Carts: $1.00   Clubs: $10.00

Amenities:

Club Pro: Tom Hale   Lessons: $40 / Lesson
Santa Clara Golf and Tennis Club offers a Practice Putting Green, a Chipping Green and a Driving Range. Bucket prices: $2.00 - $4.00. David's Restaurant is open from 6 a.m. until 11 p.m. A Cocktail Lounge and Pro Shop are available for your convenience. Reservations can be made 7 days in advance starting at 7:00 a.m. May 1st, Green Fees and Rental Fees subject to change.

Course Highlights:

Santa Clara Golf and Tennis Club opened on April 5, 1987, it is adjacent to the Santa Clara Convention Center. This is a very busy course with over 400 tournaments being played here each year. The course measures 6,822 yards from the Blue Tees, 6,457 yards from the White Tees and 5,639 yards from the Red Tees. The ratings are 72.2, 70.5 and 66.6, respectively. The course record is 66 from the Men's Tees and 67 from the Women's. This course is somewhat exposed to winds by being in the valley with few windbreaks available. This can add an interesting dimension to judging the strength of your golf swing.

Santa Teresa Golf Club

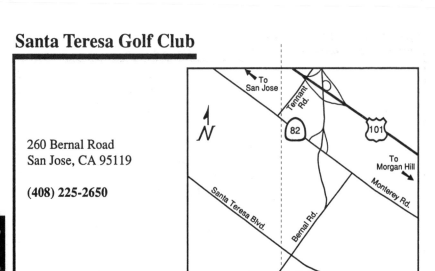

Santa Clara County

260 Bernal Road
San Jose, CA 95119

(408) 225-2650

18 Hole Course

1991 Green Fees:

	Weekdays	Weekends
9 Holes:	*$13.00	*$16.00
18 Holes:	$20.00	$28.00

Twilight Rate: Same as 9 hole fees
Senior Discount: $13 Wkdys. - Before 10 a.m., between 1&2 p.m.

Equipment Rental:

Golf Cars - 9 Holes: $11.00   Golf Cars - 18 Holes: $20.00
     Pull Carts: $3.00   Clubs: $ 6.00 / $10.00

Amenities:

Club Pro: Bob Mejias   Lessons: Variable Rate
Santa Teresa has a Practice Putting Green, Chipping Green and a
Driving Range. Bucket prices: $3.00 - $5.00. Their Bar and Grill
is open from 6 a.m. until 10 p.m. The Pro Shop carries a complete
line of merchandise. Reservations can be made starting at 8:00
a.m. on Monday for the following Saturday & Sunday. Wkdys. 7
days in advance at 6 a.m. * 9 Hole Fees apply for 1st hour in a.m.

Course Highlights:

The course opened in 1962. A new clubhouse and banquet facility
was completed in 1987. The course is a long 6,742 yards from the
Championship Tees with a par of 71. From the regular tees the
yardage comes down to 6,430 with the Women's yardage at 6,027.
The course record of 66 is held by Mitch Yeaton. The hole
selection has three par 5's at 492, 479 and a whopping 529 yards.
Even the four par 3's play long with an average length of 168.5
yards. There are doglegs galore, some having very challenging
angles. If you are walking the course it will seem longer than the
3.65 miles due to the rolling landscape.

Shoreline Golf Links

2600 North Shoreline Blvd.
Mountain View, CA 94043

(415) 969-2041

18 Hole Course

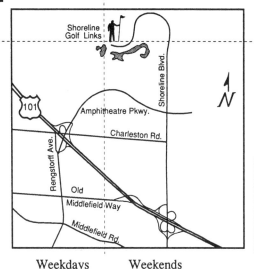

1991 Green Fees:

	Weekdays	Weekends
9 Holes:	*$17.00	*$17.00
18 Holes:	$29.00	$38.00

Twilight Rate: After 1:00 / 4:00 p.m. same as 9 hole fees
Senior Discount: $21.00 weekdays only

Equipment Rental:

Golf Cars - 9 Holes:	$10.00	Golf Cars - 18 Holes:	$20.00
Pull Carts:	$2.50	Clubs:	$12.00

Amenities:

Club Pro: Jack Guio   Lessons: $30 / 45 Minutes
A Practice Putting Green, Chipping Green and Driving Range are
all available at Shoreline Golf Links. The Snack Bar is open from
dawn to dusk. The Pro Shop carries a complete line of golf
accessories. Weekend reservations can be made on the Monday
prior at 7:00, for weekdays, 7 days in advance. *1st 1 1/2 hr. in
a.m. from back 9.

Course Highlights:

Shoreline Golf Links originally known as "Shoreline Golf Course"
opened in 1983. Located in Mountain View's Shoreline Regional
Park, the course has both a proximity to the Bay as well as a gently
rolling terrain that is typical of a traditional Scottish links course.
The course was remodelled in 1986-1987 to bring the similarity
closer. The course was originally designed and improved by
Robert Trent Jones, Jr. and Associates. Par on the course is a 72
and the length is a healthy 6,819 yards from the Pro Tees, 6,235
yards from the Men's and 5,488 yards from the Women's. Chien
Soon Lu holds the course record of 64.

Spring Valley Golf Course

3441 East Calaveras Blvd.
Milpitas, CA 95035

(408) 262-1722

18 Hole Course

1991 Green Fees:	Weekdays	Weekends
9 Holes:	n.a.	n.a.
18 Holes:	$17.00	$25/00
Twilight Rate:	$12.00	$14.00
Senior Discount:	$14.00 weekdays only	

Equipment Rental:

Golf Cars - 9 Holes:	Golf Cars - 18 Holes: $20.00
Pull Carts: $2.00	Clubs: $15.00

Amenities:

Club Pro: Richard Stewart   Lessons: $45 / 30 Minutes
Spring Valley offers both a Practice Putting Green and a Driving
Range. Bucket price: $3.00. Their restaurant is open from 8 a.m.
until 3 p.m. weekdays and 6 a.m. until 3 p.m. on weekends. A
lounge and Pro Shop are also available. Weekend reservations can
be made one week in advance in person or on Monday by calling.
Their busiest day is Friday, least busy day is Monday.

Course Highlights:

The Spring Valley Golf Course opened in 1956. This is a par 70
course for men and a par 73 for women. The course record of 62 is
held by George Bruno. The length of the course is moderate at
6,099 yards. The holes range in length from a par 5, 510 yards on
#6, down to a pair of 150 yard, par 3's, on #2 and #7. To add a bit
of a challenge, on three of the holes you tee off directly facing
water. It is a predominantly straight course with the exception of
mild doglegs, the most difficult being on the 10th at an approximate 45 degree angle.

Summit Pointe Golf Club

1200 Country Club Drive
Milpitas, CA 95035

(408) 262-8813

18 Hole Course

1991 Green Fees:

	Weekdays	Weekends
9 Holes:	n.a.	n.a.
18 Holes:	$20.00	$31.00

Twilight Rate: $10 at 3 p.m., $15 at 1 p.m.
Senior Discount: $15.00 during the week.

Equipment Rental:

Golf Cars - 9 Holes: Golf Cars - 18 Holes: $20.00
    Pull Carts: $2.00   Clubs: $10.00

Amenities:

Club Pro: Mark Dorcak   Lessons: $30 / 45 Minutes
Summit Pointe has both a Practice Putting Green and a Driving
Range. The Club at Summit Pointe is open from 7 a.m. until 9
p.m. The Pro Shop carries a full range of golf accessories.
Weekend reservations can be made on the Saturday prior beginning at 7:00 a.m. and for weekdays seven days in advance. The
busiest day of the week is Saturday, least busy day is Tuesday.

Course Highlights:

Summit Pointe opened on August 19, 1978 as "Tularcitos Golf
Course". The name was changed on October 1, 1988 to Summit
Pointe, after being newly acquired. The entire course was
renovated in 1988-1989 including the cart paths and clubhouse.
The course has a par of 72 and averages 6,000 yards in length.
From the Pro Tees the yardage is 6,311, from the Men's 6,048 and
from the Women's 5,496. The course record of 65 is held by
Estaban Toledo. The course regularly hosts the "Milpitas/
Berryessa YMCA" Tournament.

Sunken Gardens Municipal Golf Course

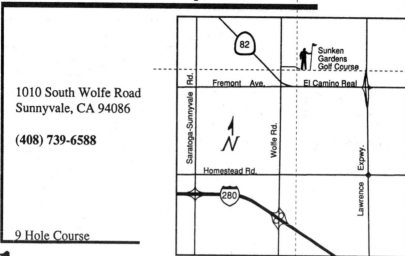

1010 South Wolfe Road
Sunnyvale, CA 94086

(408) 739-6588

Santa Clara County

9 Hole Course

1991 Green Fees:

	Weekdays	Weekends
9 Holes:	$6.25	$8.50
18 Holes:	$9.50	$13.50

Twilight Rate: Yes
Senior Discount: Sunnyvale residents only

Equipment Rental:

Golf Cars - 9 Holes:	n.a.*	Golf Cars - 18 Holes:	n.a.*
Pull Carts:	$2.00	Clubs:	$4.00

Amenities:

Club Pro: Art Wilson   Lessons: $30 / Lesson
There is a Practice Putting Green and a Driving Range available.
Bucket prices: $3.00 - $5.00. Their restaurant is open from 6:30
a.m. until 3:00 p.m. Drinks are available in the lounge. The Pro
Shop is complete. * A Golf Car is available for handicapped
persons. Weekend reservations taken on the Monday prior if
resident of Sunnyvale, otherwise on Tuesday prior.

Course Highlights:

The course is a very short par 29 at 1,586 yards. It is nestled in a
low-lying region that belies the fact it sits in the midst of several
congested roadways. The fairways are narrow and bordered by
many obstacles. Well executed iron shots are the hallmark for a
successful outing. The par 3's on #3 and #4 appear longer than
they are so be careful in choosing your club. The tee shot on #5 is
a blind shot to the flag due to a large cluster of trees. Length of
the holes will range from a long 300 yards on #6 to a short 105
yards on the 7th. Water does not play a significant role but due to
the strategic placement of several sand traps errant shots to the
greens can become most unpleasant.

Sunnyvale Municipal Golf Course

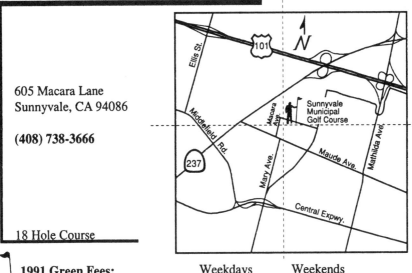

605 Macara Lane
Sunnyvale, CA 94086

(408) 738-3666

18 Hole Course

1991 Green Fees:

	Weekdays	Weekends
9 Holes:	n.a.	n.a.
18 Holes:	$13.00	$17.00
Twilight Rate: After 2 p.m.	$10.00	$13.00

Senior Discount: Sunnyvale residents only

Equipment Rental:

Golf Cars - 9 Holes:	Golf Cars - 18 Holes: $19.00
Pull Carts: $3.00	Clubs: $10.00

Amenities:

Club Pro: Art Wilson   Lessons: $25 / 30 Minutes
The course offers a Practice Putting Green but no Driving Range.
The Lookout Inn Restaurant is open from 7 a.m. until 8 p.m. Art
Wilson's Pro Shop carries a full line of golf merchandise. Weekend
reservations can be made by Sunnyvale residents on the Monday
prior starting at 6:00 a.m., non-residents on Tuesday prior starting at
7:00 a.m. No weekday reservations taken, first come, first serve.

Course Highlights:

The Sunnyvale Municipal Golf Course has been open for nineteen
years. Six of the holes were renovated in 1988. The course is 5,744
yards from the Men's Tees and 5,176 yards from the Women's Tees,
with pars of 70 and 71, respectively. The 1st and the 5th holes will
challenge you with doglegs approaching 90 degrees. The 8th green
is delicately situated with water and traps on the perimeter. Water
hazards need to be negotiated on eight of the holes. The course plays
hosts to many tournaments, including the "City of Sunnyvale
Chamber of Commerce Tournament".

Thunderbird Golf & Country Club

221 South King Road
San Jose, CA 95135

(408) 259-3355

Santa Clara County

18 Hole Course

1991 Green Fees:	Weekdays	Weekends
9 Holes:	n.a	n.a.
18 Holes:	$12.00	$14.00
Twilight Rate: After 2 p.m.	$9.00	$10.00

Senior Discount: $9.00 during the week.

Equipment Rental:

Golf Cars - 9 Holes:	Golf Cars - 18 Holes: $15.00
Pull Carts: $2.00	Clubs: $4.00

Amenities:

Club Pro: n.a.   Lessons: n.a.

There is a Practice Putting Green, Chipping Green and a Driving Range at Thunderbird Golf and Country Club. Bucket prices range from $2.50 - $4.00. Only packaged snacks available. They do not take reservations, first come, first serve.

Course Highlights:

This public, 18 hole course is not considered long at 4,802 yards, but it does have two par 5 holes at 450 yards each, and a par 4, 430 yard hole. Par for the course is a 64 for Men and a 65 for Women. The course has a rating of 58. Water will come into play on the 1st and the 9th holes, and except for slight doglegs on the 16th and 18th, the course is predominantly straight. Thunderbird Golf and Country Club is the sister to the Pleasant Hill Golf Course.

132

Copyright 1991 by Locations Plus..

Quantity Discounts Available!

For club tournaments or company golf outings the <u>Bay Area Golf Guide</u> makes a perfect gift.

Call or write for details of the attractive discounts available to your group or organization.

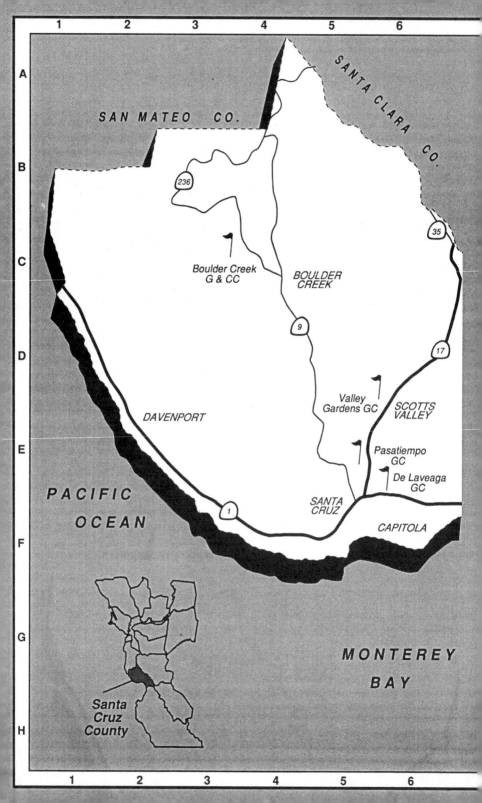

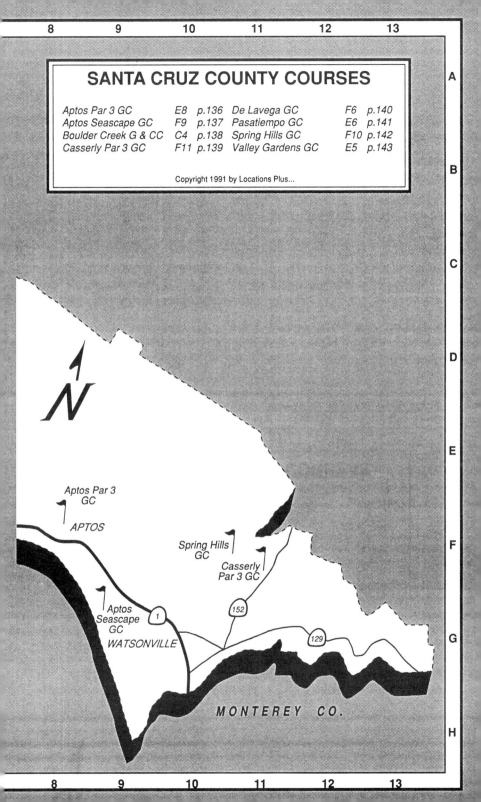

SANTA CRUZ COUNTY COURSES

Aptos Par 3 GC	E8	p.136	De Lavega GC	F6	p.140
Aptos Seascape GC	F9	p.137	Pasatiempo GC	E6	p.141
Boulder Creek G & CC	C4	p.138	Spring Hills GC	F10	p.142
Casserly Par 3 GC	F11	p.139	Valley Gardens GC	E5	p.143

N

Aptos Par 3
GC

APTOS

Spring Hills
GC

Casserly
Par 3 GC

Aptos
Seascape
GC

WATSONVILLE

1

152

129

MONTEREY CO.

Aptos Par 3

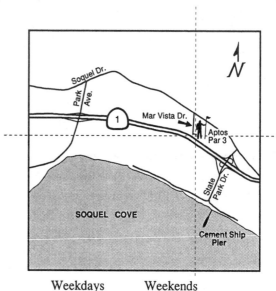

2600 Mar Vista Drive
Aptos, CA 95003

(408) 688-5000

9 Hole Course

1991 Green Fees:

	Weekdays	Weekends
9 Holes:	$5.00	$5.00
18 Holes:	$7.00	$8.00

Twilight Rate: n.a.
Senior Discount: n.a.

Equipment Rental:

Golf Cars - 9 Holes: n.a.	Golf Cars - 18 Holes:
Pull Carts: $1.00	Clubs: $4.00

Amenities:

Club Pro: Howard Menge   Lessons: $20 / 30 Minutes
Aptos Par 3 offers a Practice Putting Green and a Driving Range,
Large Bucket: $3.00, Small Bucket: $2.00. Their Pro Shop special-
izes in custom made golf clubs. A Snack Bar is available only on the
weekends. Reservations can be made at any time. Their least busy
day is Monday.

Course Highlights:

Aptos Par 3 Golf Course has been in operation since 1962. The
course plays for a total of 1,068 yards. It has a par of 27. The holes
range from a short 85 yards on the 4th hole to 150 yards on the 8th
hole. The course record stands at 22. This is a tricky course, by no
means easy. Aptos Par 3 will test your short iron game as well as
provide you with a pleasurable walk.

Aptos Seascape Golf Course

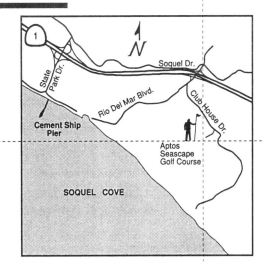

610 Clubhouse Drive
Aptos, CA 95003

(408) 688-3213

18 Hole Course

1991 Green Fees:

	Weekdays	Weekends
9 Holes:	n.a.	n.a.
18 Holes:	$25.00	$42.00
Twilight Rate:	$18.00	$27.00
Senior Discount:	n.a.	

Equipment Rental:

Golf Cars - 9 Holes:	Golf Cars - 18 Holes: $22.00
Pull Carts: $3.00	Clubs: $15.00

Amenities:

Club Pro: Don Elser   Lessons: $30 / 30 Minutes
This course offers 2 Practice Putting Greens, a Chipping Green and a Driving Range. Bucket prices: $2.25 - $4.50. They have a full restaurant and a Snack Bar available for your convenience. Weekend reservations can be made on the Monday prior, beginning at 10:00 a.m. and for weekday play, 7 days in advance beginning at 7:30 a.m. Their busiest day is Friday their least busy day is Tuesday.

Course Highlights:

Aptos Seascape Golf Course originally opened as a 9 hole course in 1926 and was known as Rio Del Mar Country Club. It was expanded to 18 holes in late 1929. The course changed names two more times before 1986 when it was purchased by the American Golf Corporation. They renovated the pro shop and restaurant and installed a fully automatic irrigation system on the course. This is a beautiful course, tree lined, with rolling fairways. Total Men's yardage is 6,123, and Women's yardage is 5,656. Overall par is 72.

137

Boulder Creek Golf & Country Club

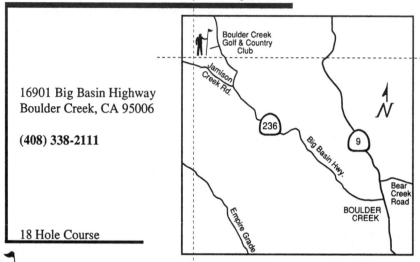

16901 Big Basin Highway
Boulder Creek, CA 95006

(408) 338-2111

18 Hole Course

1991 Green Fees:

	Weekdays	Weekends
9 Holes:	n.a.	n.a.
18 Holes:	$16.00	$26.00
Twilight Rate:	$12.00	$16.00
Senior Discount:	$11.00 Monday through Friday	

Equipment Rental:

Golf Cars - 9 Holes:	n.a.	Golf Cars - 18 Holes:	$16.00
Pull Carts:	n.a.	Clubs:	$8.00

Amenities:

Club Pro: Hal Wells   Lessons: $30 / Lesson
Boulder Creek has a Practice Putting Green and a Chipping Green,
but no Driving Range. A Pro Shop, with limited merchandise, is
open for your convenience. The Redwood Room, restaurant and
lounge is open from 9 a.m. to 3 p.m. weekdays, and 7 a.m. to 3 p.m.
on weekends. All reservations can be made seven days in advance.

Course Highlights:

This course opened with 9 holes in 1961 and 9 more were added in
1966. The course was designed by Jack Fleming. It winds its way
around homes and condominiums and insists on the golfers being
pretty much on target. The course has been steadily improved and it
is a pleasure to play. Men's and Women's course ratings are 61.3.
Total yardage for the Men is 4,279, par is 65, Women's yardage is
3,970, par 65.

138

Casserly Par 3 Golf Course

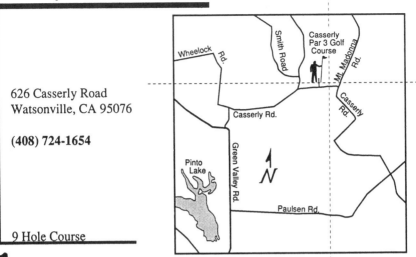

626 Casserly Road
Watsonville, CA 95076

(408) 724-1654

9 Hole Course

1991 Green Fees:

	Weekdays	Weekends
9 Holes:	$3.50	$4.00
18 Holes:	$7.00	$8.00

Twilight Rate: n.a.
Senior Discount: n.a.

Equipment Rental:

Golf Cars - 9 Holes: n.a.   Golf Cars - 18 Holes: n.a.
Pull Carts: $ .50   Clubs: $3.00

Amenities:

Club Pro: n.a.   Lessons: n.a.
Casserly Par 3 Golf Course has a Practice Putting Green, but no
Chipping Green or Driving Range. Their Pro Shop carries a limited
amount of golf accessories. Candy bars and other such snacks are
available along with soft beverages.

Course Highlights:

Casserly Par 3 Golf Course opened in 1966. This course has two sets
of tees, one for the front 9 holes, and one for the back 9. Total
yardage for 18 holes is 2,422, par 54. The longest hole would be
#15, which is a straight shot to the green. There are two water holes,
one on #6 in the middle of the fairway and the other on #5 just right
of the green. The course record for playing 9 holes is 22 from the
front tees, and 23 from the back tees.

139

De Laveaga Golf Course

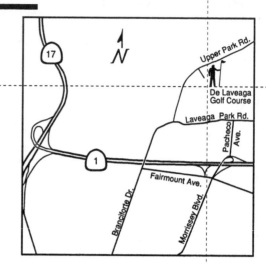

401 Upper Park Road
Santa Cruz, CA 95060

(408) 423-7212

18 Hole Course

1991 Green Fees:

	Weekdays	Weekends
9 Holes:	$13.00	$18.00
18 Holes:	$18.50	$25.00
Twilight Rate:	$12.00	$16.50

Senior Discount: With county resident cards.

Equipment Rental:

Golf Cars - 9 Holes: Golf Cars - 18 Holes: $22.00

Pull Carts: $3.00   Clubs: $15.00

Amenities:

Club Pro: Gary Loustalot   Lessons: $35 / 30 Minutes
This course offers a Practice Putting Green, Chipping Green and a
Driving Range. Buckets range from $3 to $5. Full clubhouse
facilities from 7 to 2 and the Snack Bar is open from 7 to 4. Reservations for weekdays can be made on the Sunday prior at 2:00 p.m. and
for the weekends on the Monday prior beginning at 7:00 a.m.

Course Highlights:

This 18 hole course winds its way through the Santa Cruz Mountains.
It is not a long course, it measures 6,010 from the Men's Tees and
only 5,346 from the Women's Tees, but for sure it is a challenge.
Balls hit too long or too far off course will be lost forever. If you
enjoy a mountain outing you will enjoy De Laveaga. Par for the
course is 72. The Men's rating is 70.1, slope 130, Ladies is 70.7,
slope 126.

140

Pasatiempo Golf Course

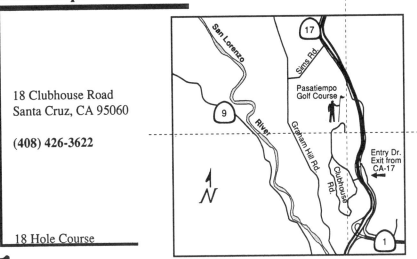

18 Clubhouse Road
Santa Cruz, CA 95060

(408) 426-3622

18 Hole Course

1991 Green Fees:

	Weekdays	Weekends
9 Holes:	n.a.	n.a.
18 Holes:	$60.00	*$70.00
Twilight Rate: After 2 p.m.	$33.00	$39.00
Senior Discount: n.a.	*Fri. considered to be weekend	

Equipment Rental:

Golf Cars - 9 Holes: $16.00	Golf Cars - 18 Holes: $25.00
Pull Carts: $5.00	Clubs: $20.00

Amenities:

Club Pro: Shawn McEntee   Lessons: $30 / 30 Minutes
Pasatiempo Golf Club offers a Practice Putting Green, Chipping Green and a Driving Range. Bucket prices: $2.00 - $4.00. The Hollins House Restaurant is open daily. They are in the process of building a new clubhouse. The Pro Shop carries a complete line of golf accessories. Weekend reservations can be made on the Monday prior beginning at 10:00 a.m., weekdays seven days in advance.

Course Highlights:

Marion Hollins, a U.S. Women's Amateur Champion, purchased the 600 rolling acres near Monterey Bay and commissioned Dr. Alister Mackenzie, a golf course architect from Scotland, to design Pasatiempo which was completed in 1929. This championship course hosts the Western Intercollegiate Tournament each spring and it has done so for the past 40 years. The ratings are: Championship 72.3, Regular 70.9 and Ladies 72.6. A trip to Pasatiempo for a round of golf should prove to be most enjoyable.

141

Spring Hills Golf Course

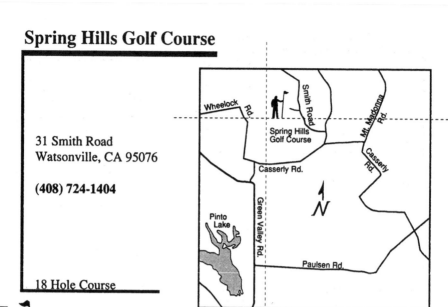

31 Smith Road
Watsonville, CA 95076

(408) 724-1404

18 Hole Course

1991 Green Fees:

	Weekdays	Weekends
9 Holes:	n.a.	n.a.
18 Holes:	$15.00	$20.00

Twilight Rate: After 2:00 / 3:00 $10 weekdays
Senior Discount: n.a.

Equipment Rental:

Golf Cars - 9 Holes: $10.00   Golf Cars - 18 Holes: $20.00
     Pull Carts: $2.00 / $3.00   Clubs: n.a.

Amenities:

Club Pro: n.a.   Lessons: *
This course offers a Practice Putting Green, Chipping Green and a
Driving Range. Medium Bucket: $2.00. Their Snack Bar is open
from 8 a.m. until 5 p.m., beer is available. The Pro Shop carries the
standard necessities. *Lessons are by appointment only. They do
take reservations.

Course Highlights:

Spring Hills Golf Course opened in 1965 and has steadily
increased in popularity. It is nestled at the base of the foothills which
provides protection from the wind, besides a lovely location. The
course is rated 68.7 for the Men, and 71.1 for the Women. Men's
yardage is 6,281, par 71, and Women's yardage is 5,428, par 71.

142

Valley Gardens Golf Course

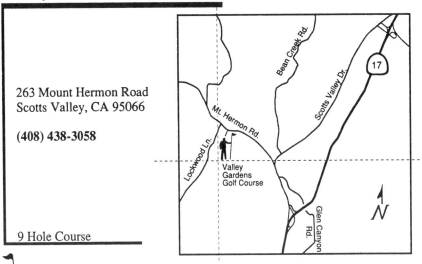

263 Mount Hermon Road
Scotts Valley, CA 95066

(408) 438-3058

9 Hole Course

1991 Green Fees:

	Weekdays	Weekends
9 Holes:	$7.00	$8.00
18 Holes:	$13.00	$15.00

Twilight Rate: n.a.
Senior Discount: Limited to Wednesdays

Equipment Rental:

Golf Cars - 9 Holes:	n.a.	Golf Cars - 18 Holes:	n.a.
Pull Carts:	$1.50	Clubs:	$4.00

Amenities:

Club Pro: Jerry Imel   Lessons: 5 for $85
This course offers a Practice Putting Green, but no Chipping Green
or Driving Range. A limited Snack Bar is available. Their Pro Shop
is presently being expanded. Reservations for weekends can be
made the prior Saturday or Sunday. Their least busy day of the week
is Tuesday.

Course Highlights:

Valley Gardens Golf Course is a short course measuring 1,765 yards
from the Men's Tees and 1,557 yards from the Ladies' Tees. A short
course, but none the less a challenging one. Four of the holes have
water hazards, on the 8th hole you must drive over one to reach the
green. This is a beautiful, well manicured, tree lined course. They
boast that their greens are the best in county. Par for the course is 31.
It is rated 56.5 from the Men's Tees and 55 from the Ladies' Tees.

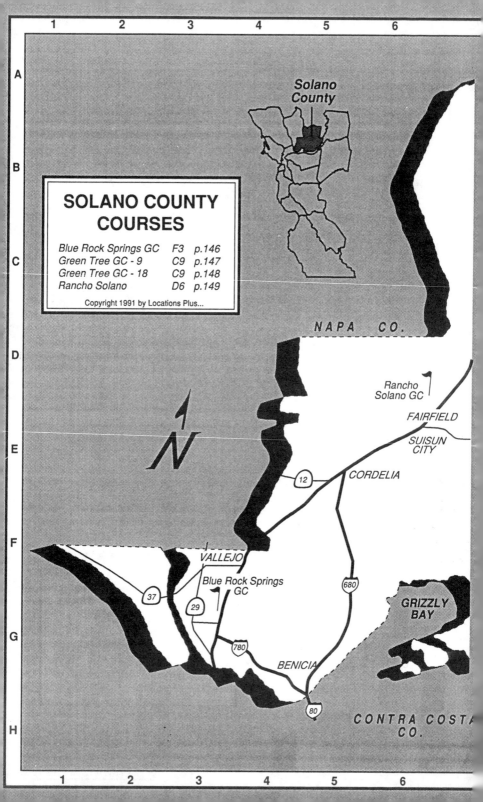

SOLANO COUNTY COURSES

Copyright 1991 by Locations Plus...

Solano County

NAPA CO.

Rancho Solano GC

FAIRFIELD

SUISUN CITY

N

12

CORDELIA

VALLEJO

Blue Rock Springs GC

37

29

680

GRIZZLY BAY

780

BENICIA

80

CONTRA COSTA CO.

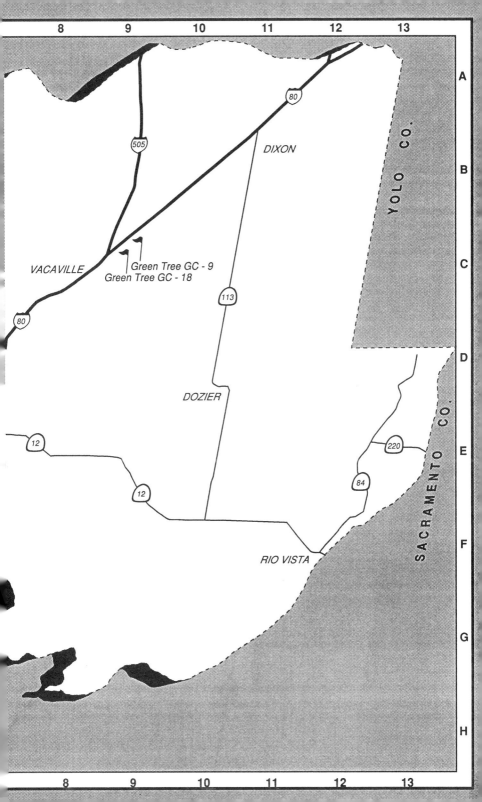

Blue Rock Springs Municipal Golf Course

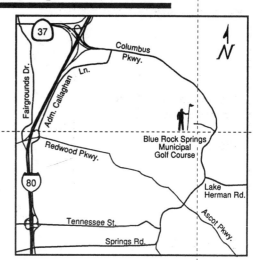

Columbus Parkway
Vallejo, CA 94590

(707) 643-8476

18 Hole Course

1991 Green Fees

	Weekdays	Weekends
9 Holes:	n.a.	n.a
18 Holes:	$8.00	$11.00
Twilight Rate:	$4.00	$5.00
Senior Discount: n.a.		

Equipment Rental:

Golf Cars - 9 Holes:	Golf Cars - 18 Holes: $14.00
Pull Carts: $2.25	Clubs: $4.25

Amenities:

Club Pro: Ralph W. Harris   Lessons: $20.00 / Lesson
Blue Rock Municipal Golf Course offers a Practice Putting Green
and a Chipping Green but no Driving Range. The Rentrows Coffee
Shop is open from 6 a.m. until 7 p.m. for your convenience. Their
Pro Shop carries a full line of golf merchandise. Weekend reservations can be made on the prior Tuesday, for weekdays they can be
made seven days in advance.

Course Highlights:

In 1938 Blue Rock Municipal opened as a 9 hole course, in 1946 it
was expanded to 18 holes. Yardage from the Men's Tees is 6,091,
par 72, and 5,894 yards from the Ladies' Tees, par 73. Course
ratings, Men's: 69.4, Ladies': 72.7. The course record is held by Jeff
Wilson with a 63. The course regularly hosts the Joe Brophy Jr.
Tournament and the Vallejo City Championship Tournament.

Green Tree Golf Course - 9

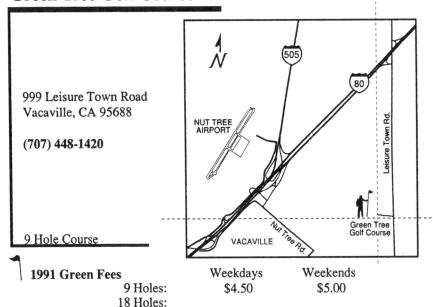

999 Leisure Town Road
Vacaville, CA 95688

(707) 448-1420

9 Hole Course

1991 Green Fees

	Weekdays	Weekends
9 Holes:	$4.50	$5.00
18 Holes:		
Twilight Rate:		
Senior Discount: $1.00 off regular Green Fees		

Equipment Rental:

Golf Cars - 9 Holes: $10.00   Golf Cars - 18 Holes:
   Pull Carts: $2.00   Clubs: $5.00

Amenities:

Club Pro: Kelly Adams   Lessons: $20 / 45 Minutes
This 9 hole course at Green Tree has a Practice Putting Green,
Chipping Green and a Driving Range. Large Bucket: $3.50, Small
Bucket: $1.50. Their Snack Bar is open from 6 a.m. until 8 p.m.
daily, assorted beverages are sold. The Pro Shop carries a complete
line of golf accessories. Reservations can be made one week in
advance. Their busiest day is Friday, least busy Thursday.

Course Highlights:

Green Tree Golf Course is 25 years old and originally consisted of
only 3 holes. Now this 9 hole public course is 1,053 yards long, par
is 29. It is a varied 9 holes, the longest is 260 yards and the shortest
is 113 yards. This is a beautifully maintained course which offers
you a chance to warm-up for the longer Green Tree 18 hole course.
It is also an excellent course to help you perfect those short iron
shots. It is not a strenuous course to walk for it is relatively flat.

Solano County

147

Green Tree Golf Course - 18

999 Leisure Town Rd.
Vacaville, CA 95688

(707) 448-1420

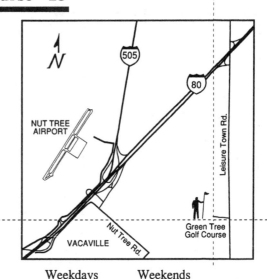

18 Hole Course

1991 Green Fees

	Weekdays	Weekends
9 Holes:	n.a.	n.a.
18 Holes:	$9.00	$13.00
Twilight Rate:	$5.50	$6.50
Senior Discount: $1.00 off		

Equipment Rental:

Golf Cars - 9 Holes:		Golf Cars - 18 Holes:	$15.00
Pull Carts:	$2.00	Clubs:	$5.00

Amenities:

Club Pro: Kelly Adams   Lessons: $20 / 45 Minutes
This 18 hole course at Green Tree has a Practice Putting Green,
Chipping Green and a Driving Range. Bucket prices: $1.50 - $3.50.
Their Snack Bar is open from 6 a.m. until 8 p.m. daily, assorted
beverages are sold. The Pro Shop carries a complete line of golf
accessories. Reservations can be made one week in advance. Their
busiest day is Friday, least busy Thursday.

Course Highlights:

Green Tree Golf Course is 25 years old and originally consisted of
only 3 holes. This 18 hole course has three sets of tees. From the
Blue Championship Tees total yardage is 6,370, from the Men's
White Tees it is 5,906 and from the Red Ladies' Tees it is 5,318.
Course ratings are: 69.1, 67.1 and 68.2 respectively. Overall par for
the course is 71. This course fits in the middle between being
difficult and easy. It is mostly flat presenting good lies. The
fairways are wide, cutting down the possibility of hitting the trees
which line most of the fairways. There are approximately 6 holes
posing water hazards. The greens are beautifully maintained.

148

Solano
County

Rancho Solano

3250 Rancho Solano Pkwy.
Fairfield, CA 94533

(707 429-4653

18 Hole Course

1991 Green Fees

	Weekdays	Weekends
9 Holes:	n.a.	n.a.
18 Holes:	$15.00	$20.00
Twilight Rate: 9 Holes	$7.50	$10.00
Senior Discount: n.a.		

Equipment Rental:

Golf Cars - 9 Holes: $10.00	Golf Cars - 18 Holes: $17/$19
Pull Carts: $3.00	Clubs: $10.00

Amenities:

Club Pro: Jeff Wilson   Lessons: $25 / 30 Minutes
This 18 hole course has a Practice Putting Green, Chipping Green
and a Driving Range. Bucket prices range from $2 to $5. There is a
full restaurant, lounge and snack bar available. Their Pro Shop's
inventory is extensive. Reservations can be made 7 days in advance,
beginning at 6:00 a.m. Their least busy time is early on weekdays.

Course Highlights:

This beautiful course, designed by Gary Roger Baird, Inc. opened on
March 3, 1990. The layout of the course you will find interesting as
well as challenging. There is no lack of sand or water. Their greens
are tremendous in size, undulating and quick. Residential property
surround portions of the course. Overall Par is 72. Yardages range
from 5,206 from the Ladies' Tees to 6,705 from the Championship
Tees. The ratings and slopes are: Blue 72.9 /129, White 70.7 / 125,
Gold 68.5 /120 and Red 69.6 /117. There are 4 par 3 holes, 10 par 4
holes and 4 par 5 holes.

Solano County

149

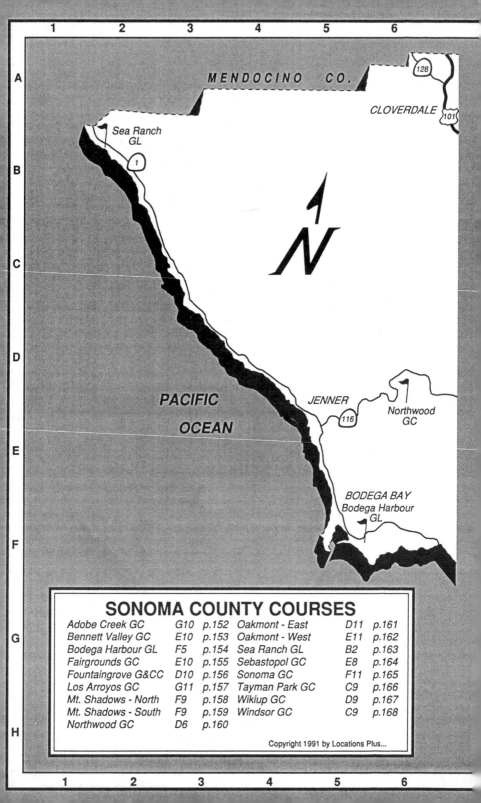

SONOMA COUNTY COURSES

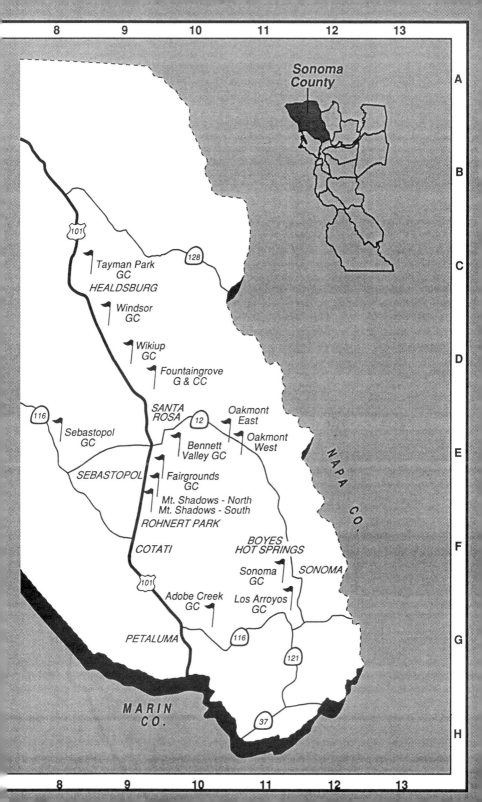

Adobe Creek Golf Club

1901 Frates Road
Petaluma, CA 94954

(707) 765-3000

18 Hole Course

A map showing the location of Adobe Creek Golf Club, with roads including E. Washington St., Adobe Rd., Manor Rd., Ely Rd., Casa Grande Rd., Frates Rd., McDowell Rd., South Ely Rd., Lakeville Hwy., Hwy 101 and Hwy 116.

1991 Green Fees:

	Weekdays	Weekends
9 Holes:	n.a.	n.a.
18 Holes:	$45.00	$55.00

Twilight Rates:
Senior Discount: n.a.

Equipment Rental: Golf Car included in Green Fee

Golf Cars - 9 Holes: Golf Cars - 18 Holes:
Pull Carts: n.a.   Clubs: $10.00

Amenities:

Club Pro: Roger Ullo   Lessons: $25 / 30 Minutes
Adobe Creek offers a Practice Putting Green, Chipping Green and a
Driving Range. Bucket prices: $2.50 - $3.00. There is a full
restaurant and lounge available. Restaurant hours: 7:00 a.m. until
6:00 p.m. A Pro shop provides a good selection of golf equipment.
Reservations can be made 2 weeks in advance. Saturday is their
busiest day of the week, Tuesday their least.

Course Highlights:

This new 18 hole course, designed by Robert Trent Jones, II opened
on July 28, 1990. It is a links style course, mounds with smooth fast
greens, the fairways are narrow, and well defined. From the four tee
choices available, the yardages range from 6,825 to 5,027. The
ratings and slopes are: Gold 72.9/132, Blue 70.1/127, White 67.6/121
and Red 68.3/115. Par for the Course is 72. Water will come into
play on 8 of the holes. This new championship course is worth a
visit.

Sonoma County

Bennett Valley Golf Course

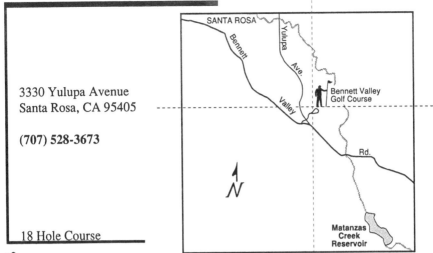

3330 Yulupa Avenue
Santa Rosa, CA 95405

(707) 528-3673

18 Hole Course

1991 Green Fees:

	Weekdays	Weekends
9 Holes:	$6.00	$8.00
18 Holes:	$9.00	$12.00

Twilight Rates: Same as 9 Hole Fee after 2:00 p.m.
Senior Discount: $6.00 weekdays only, no holidays.

Equipment Rental:

Golf Cars - 9 Holes: Golf Cars - 18 Holes: $16.00
     Pull Carts: $2.00   Clubs: $8.00

Amenities:

Club Pro: Bob Borowicz   Lessons: $22 / 30 Minutes
Bennett Valley offers a Practice Putting Green, Chipping Green and
a Driving Range. Bucket prices: $1.50 - $3.00.. Their cafe is open
from sunrise until 4 p.m. daily, a cocktail lounge is also available.
The Golf Shop carries a full line of merchandise. Weekend reservations can be made on the prior Saturday beginning at daybreak, for
weekdays one week in advance.

Course Highlights:

Any level of golfer will find this eighteen hole championship course
in Santa Rosa challenging. It is rated 70.6 from the Championship
Blue Tees, 69.0 from the White Tees, and 72.5 from the Red Tees,
Slope: 116. The course plays for a total of 6,583 yards. Men's par is
72, Ladies' par is 75. The course record stands at 61. You will
encounter water hazards on holes #1, 7, 15, and 16. Bennett Valley
Golf Course regularly hosts the Santa Rosa City Championship, both
Adult and Junior.

Sonoma
County

Bodega Harbour Golf Links

21301 Heron Drive
Bodega Bay, CA 94923

(707) 875-3538

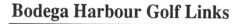

18 Hole Course

1991 Green Fees:

	Weekdays	Weekends
9 Holes:	$18.00	$30.00
18 Holes:	$35.00	$50.00

Twilight Rates: n.a.
Senior Discount: n.a.

Equipment Rental: Golf Car fee based on each player
Golf Cars - 9 Holes: $8.00   Golf Cars - 18 Holes: $12.50
Pull Carts: $3.00   Clubs: $20.00

Amenities:

Club Pro: Dennis Kalkowski   Lessons: $35 / Lesson
A Practice Putting Green is available for warm-up at Bodega
Harbour Golf Links, but no Driving Range or Chipping Green. They
have a full restaurant and lounge open daily. The Pro Shop carries a
full line of golf equipment. Reservations can be made 60 days in
advance.

Course Highlights:

This Championship golf course was designed by Robert Trent Jones,
Jr. It originally opened as a nine hole course in 1976. The second
nine was completed in September of 1987. Golf Digest nominated
this course for "Best New Resort Course - 1988." There are 3
separate sets of Tees for each of the 18 holes. Yardages range from
6,220 from the Championship Tees to 4,746 yards from the Red
Forward Tees. Ratings and slopes are: Championship 71.6 / 130,
Middle Tees 68.0 / 125 and Forward Tees 68.7 / 120. Each year it
plays host to the North Coast Amateur Tournament. You will enjoy
the unique style of this Scottish links course.

Sonoma County

154

Fairgrounds Golf Course

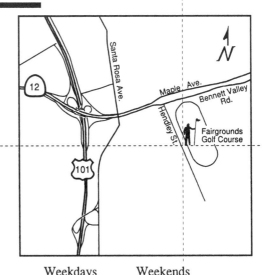

1350 Bennett Valley Road
Santa Rosa, CA 95404

(707) 546-2469

9 Hole Course

1991 Green Fees:

	Weekdays	Weekends
9 Holes:	$5.00	$6.00
18 Holes:	$6.00	$7.00
Twilight Rates: After 5:00	$3.50	$4.00
Senior Discount:	$4.00	$5.00

Equipment Rental:

Golf Cars - 9 Holes: Golf Cars - 18 Holes: n.a.
Pull Carts: $2.00   Clubs: $4.00

Amenities:

Club Pro: Wade Miller   Lessons: $30 / 60 Minutes
The Fairgrounds Golf Course offers a Practice Putting Green,
Chipping Green and a Driving Range. Large Bucket: $3.00, Small
Bucket: $2.00. Their Snack Bar is open from 7 a.m. until dark.
Monthly Green Fee rates are available.   The Pro Shop will help you
in filling any of your golfing needs. Reservations are not taken, first
come, first serve.

Course Highlights:

Fairgrounds Golf Course opened in 1956. This is a public nine hole
golf course. It measures 1,657 yards with a par of 29. There are two
par 4 holes and the rest are par 3's. This is a flat course with two
water hazards. What makes this course difficult are the small greens,
presenting small targets. You can leave your sandwedge at home, it
won't get any attention while playing this course. They have done
some upgrading of their course during the past year.

Sonoma
County

155

Fountaingrove Resort & Country Club

1525 Fountaingrove Pkwy.
Santa Rosa, CA 95403

(707) 579-4653

18 Hole Course

1991 Green Fees:	Weekdays	Weekends
9 Holes:	n.a.	n.a.
18 Holes:	$45.00	$65.00

Twilight Rates: n.a.
Senior Discount: n.a.

Equipment Rental: Golf Fee includes mandatory golf car.

Golf Cars - 9 Holes: Golf Cars - 18 Holes:
Pull Carts: n.a.   Clubs: $10.00

Amenities:

Club Pro: J. Michael Jonas   Lessons: $30 / 60 Minutes
There is a Practice Putting Green and a Driving Range available at
Fountaingrove. The Sonoma Grill, a full service restaurant and
lounge, and a Snack Bar are available. The Pro Shop is fully
stocked. Reservations can be made seven days in advance beginning
at 7:30 a.m. Their busiest day of the week is Saturday, least busy on
Monday and Tuesday.

Course Highlights:

This course, designed by Ted Robinson, opened in May of 1985.
This is a semi-private, eighteen hole championship course located on
the historic Fountaingrove Ranch. This is a very hilly course,
beautifully landscaped with plenty of trees. It also has a fairly large
lake sitting right in the center, so water will come into play on four of
the holes. From the Blue Championship Tees it is 6,797 yards, from
the White tees it is 6,380 yards and from the Red Tees it is 5,644
yards long. Course ratings are 72.8 / slope 132, 70.9 / slope 128 and
72.6, respectively. They say you will use every club in your bag by
the time you complete a round of golf at Fountaingrove.

156

Los Arroyos Golf Course

5000 Stage Gulch Road
Sonoma, CA 95476

(707) 938-2868

9 Hole Course

1991 Green Fees:

	Weekdays	Weekends
9 Holes:	$5.00	$8.00
18 Holes:	$5.00	$8.00

Twilight Rates: $3.00
Senior Discount: Wednesday - all day play

Equipment Rental:

Golf Cars - 9 Holes: n.a.   Golf Cars - 18 Holes: n.a.
    Pull Carts: $3.00   Clubs: $3.00

Amenities:

Club Pro: Gary Williams   Lessons: $30 / 60 Minutes
There is a Practice Putting Green and a Driving Range offered by
Los Arroyos Golf Course. The price of a Bucket of balls is $3.00.
The "10th Hole" is open from 7 a.m. until 7 p.m. The Pro Shop
carries a full line of golf equipment. Weekend reservations can be
made on the Friday prior and weekday reservations one day in
advance. Their busiest day is Thursday, least busy on Friday.

Course Highlights:

This semi-private 9 hole course opened in 1971. This course plays
for 1,600 yards and has a par of 29. There are two par 4's and the
rest are par 3's. The course is mostly flat and enhanced by many
Willow and Pine trees. There is a lovely creek running toward the
back of the course and a nice size lake sitting right in the middle.
The fairways are 25 yards wide, the greens are small and rolling.
Most golfers will find this little course a challenge.

Sonoma County

Mountain Shadows Resort North Course

100 Golf Course Drive
Rohnert Park, CA 94928

(707) 584-7766

18 Hole Course

1991 Green Fees:	Weekdays	Weekends
9 Holes:	n.a.	n.a.
18 Holes:	$18.00	$30.00

Twilight Rates: $15.00 - Winter 1:00 p.m. / Summer 4:00 p.m.
Senior Discount: $15.00

Equipment Rental:

Golf Cars - 9 Holes:	Golf Cars - 18 Holes: $22.00
Pull Carts: $3.00	Clubs: $10.00

Amenities:

Club Pro: Greg Anderson   Lessons: $20 / Lesson
A Practice Putting Green and a Driving Range are available at
Mountain Shadows Golf Courses. Large Bucket: $3.50. Their
restaurant is open from 6 a.m. until 9 p.m., a cocktail lounge is also
available. The Pro Shop carries a full line of golf equipment.
Reservations can be made one week in advance. Their busiest day
of the week is Friday, least busy day is Monday.

Course Highlights:

This eighteen hole championship golf course has 4 separate sets of
tee boxes. From the designated Tournament Gold Tees there is a
total of 7,035 yards and is rated 72.1. From the Championship Blue
Tees the course is 6,690 yards long and is rated 69.7. From the
Regular White Tees the course plays for 6,160 yards and it is rated
67.5. The yardage from the Red Tees, is 5,503 yards long and is
rated 70.4. There is a bit of a challenge to meet on almost all of the
holes. Polish up the clubs and come out swinging. This is the North
Course at Mountain Shadows, there is also a South Course.

Mountain Shadows Resort South Course

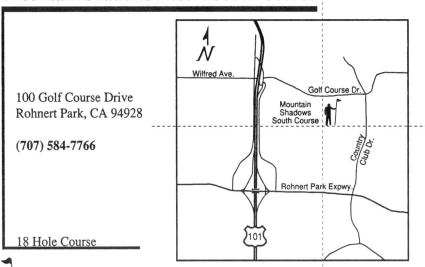

100 Golf Course Drive
Rohnert Park, CA 94928

(707) 584-7766

18 Hole Course

1991 Green Fees:

	Weekdays	Weekends
9 Holes:	n.a.	n.a.
18 Holes:	$16.00	$25.00

Twilight Rates: $13.00 - Winter 1:00 p.m. / Summer 4:00 p.m.
Senior Discount: $13.00

Equipment Rental:

Golf Cars - 9 Holes:	Golf Cars - 18 Holes: $22.00
Pull Carts: $3.00	Clubs: $10.00

Amenities:

Club Pro: Greg Anderson   Lessons: $25/ Lesson
A Practice Putting Green and Driving Range are available at Mountain Shadows. Large Bucket: $3.50. Their restaurant is open from 6 a.m. until 9 p.m. The Pro Shop carries a full line of golf equipment. Reservations can be made one week in advance. Their busiest day of the week is Friday, least busy day is Monday.

Course Highlights:

Mountain Shadows Golf Course - South is one of the two 18 hole courses available here. This course, in comparison to the North course, is a little more difficult, as the fairways are quite narrow. The course has been newly renovated by installing a new irrigation system and cart paths. Total yardage for the course is 6,500, par 72. The course is rated 69.7.

Sonoma County

159

Northwood Golf Course

19400 Highway 116
Monte Rio, CA 95462

(707) 865-1116

9 Hole Course

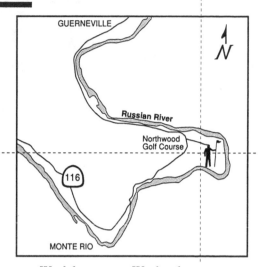

1991 Green Fees:

	Weekdays	Weekends
9 Holes:	$11.00	$14.00
18 Holes:	$17.00	$22.00

Twilight Rates: $6.00
Senior Discount: 10 rounds for $80.00 Monday thru Friday

Equipment Rental:

Golf Cars - 9 Holes: $10.00		Golf Cars - 18 Holes: $16.00
Pull Carts: $1.50		Clubs: $4.00

Amenities:

Club Pro: Staff   Lessons: $15 / 30 Minutes
Northwood Golf Course offers a Practice Putting Green, Chipping
Green and a Driving Range as their warm-up facilities. The North-
wood Restaurant and Lounge is open from 10 a.m. until 10 p.m. The
Pro Shop will be able to fill your golfing needs. Reservations can be
made two weeks in advance. Their busiest day of the week is
Saturday, least busy day is Tuesday.

Course Highlights:

Northwood Golf Course was designed by the famed golf course
architect, Alister Mackenzie in 1928. During the 1950's this course
played host to such notables as Bing Crosby, Phil Harris and Lowell
Thomas. The course is situated in close proximity to the renowned
Bohemian Club. This nine hole course runs for a total of 2,875 yards
and has a par of 36. Northwood is located up in the scenic wine
country. Huge Redwood and Oak trees lining the narrow fairways
make you feel as if you are out for a pleasurable walk in the woods.

Oakmont Golf Club East

565 Oak Vista Court
Santa Rosa, CA 95405

(707) 538-2454

18 Hole Course

1991 Green Fees:

	Weekdays	Weekends
9 Holes:	$11.00	$14.00
18 Holes:	$15.00	$20.00

Twilight Rates: 9 Hole Fee at 2:00 p.m.
Senior Discount: n.a.

Equipment Rental:

Golf Cars - 9 Holes:	Golf Cars - 18 Holes: $20.00
Pull Carts: $3.00	Clubs: $5.00

Amenities:

Club Pro: Lessons:

The amenities offered by Oakmont will be found at Oakmont - West. There is a small Pro Shop located here with a very limited supply of golf accessories. The only refreshments are provided by vending machines. Reservations can be made one week in advance after 6:30 a.m. The busiest day of the week is Friday, least busy day is Tuesday.

Course Highlights:

Oakmont - East was the first 18 hole golf course to open at the Oakmont Golf Club. This is the shorter of the two courses measuring 4,293 yards from the Men's Tees. It plays for a total of 4,067 yards from the Ladie's Tees. Overall par is 63. The course rating from the White Tees is 58.5 and from the Red Tees, 62.2, slope is 94. This course is located in what is regionally known as the "Valley of the Moon." Homes have been built in recent years that surround most of the golf course.

Sonoma County

161

Oakmont Golf Club West

7025 Oakmont Drive
Santa Rosa, CA 95405

(707) 539-0415

18 Hole Course

1991 Green Fees:

	Weekdays	Weekends
9 Holes:	$13.00	$18.00
18 Holes:	$20.00	$28.00

Twilight Rates: 9 Hole Fee at 2:00 p.m.
Senior Discount: n.a.

Equipment Rental:

Golf Cars - 9 Holes:	Golf Cars - 18 Holes: $20.00
Pull Carts: $3.00	Clubs: $5.00

Amenities:

Club Pro: Dean James   Lessons: $20 / 30 Minutes
Oakmont Golf Course - West offers a Practice Putting Green and a
Driving Range. Large Bucket: $2.50, Small Bucket: $1.50. The
Chalet at Oakmont is open from 11 a.m. until 3 p.m. and from 5 p.m.
until 8 p.m. A cocktail lounge is also available. The Pro Shop carries
a complete line of golf equipment. Reservations for the weekends
can be made one week in advance beginning at 6.30 p.m.

Course Highlights:

Oakmont Golf Course - West was the second 18 hole course to
be constructed at the Oakmont Golf Club. This is their Championship Course which each year features the Woodstock Open, host ,
Charles Shultz. Yardage from the Blue Tees is 6,417, from the
White Tees it is 6,048 and the Red Tees it is 5,506. Course Ratings
are: 70.7, 68.7 and 70.7, respectively. Slope: 116-112. This is the
more difficult of the Oakmont Courses located here in the "Valley of
the Moon."

Sonoma County

The Sea Ranch Golf Links

49300 Hwy. 1
Sea Ranch, CA 95497

(707) 785-2467

9 Hole Course

1991 Green Fees:

	Weekdays	Weekends
9 Holes:	$15.00	$20.00
18 Holes:	$20.00	$30.00

Twilight Rates: n.a.
Senior Discount: n.a.

Equipment Rental:

Golf Cars - 9 Holes: $12.00   Golf Cars - 18 Holes: $20.00
Pull Carts: $2.00   Clubs: $15.00 / $25.00

Amenities:

Club Pro: Rich Bland   Lessons: $30 / 30 Minutes
The Sea Ranch Golf Links offers a Practice Putting Green and a
Driving Range. Large Bucket: $6.00, Small Bucket: $3.00. The Sea
Ranch Lodge Restaurant is open daily for your convenience. The
Pro Shop offers a nice selection of golfing equipment. Reservations
can be made 30 days in advance.

Course Highlights:

This 9 hole course, designed by Robert Muir Graves, was constructed in 1973. The course measures 6,740 yards and has a par of
73 when playing 18 holes. It also provides three sets of tees. The
course is rated 73.5 and has a slope of 133, the 13th highest in
Northern California. The course record is held by Rich Bland with a
69. In 1991 Golf Digest rated Sea Ranch Golf Links as one of the
Top 5, 9 hole golf courses in Northern California.

Sonoma
County

163

Sebastopol Golf Course

2881 Scotts Right of Way
Sebastopol, CA 95472

(707) 823-9852

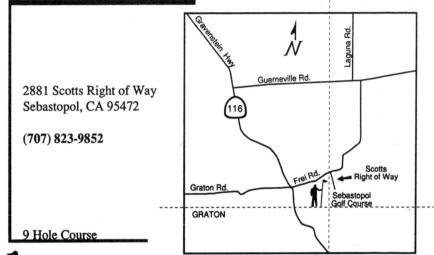

9 Hole Course

1991 Green Fees:

	Weekdays	Weekends
9 Holes:	$7.00	$9.00
18 Holes:	$8.00	$10.00

Twilight Rates: n.a.
Senior Discount: $6.00 Wednesday only

Equipment Rental:

Golf Cars - 9 Holes: $7.00   Golf Cars - 18 Holes: $10.00
     Pull Carts: $2.00   Clubs: $3.00

Amenities:

Club Pro: Lee Farris   Lessons: n.a.
Sebastopol Golf Course has a Practice Putting Green, but no Chipping Green or Driving Range. The Snack Bar is open from dawn to dusk for your convenience. The Pro Shop carries sufficient equipment to help fill your golfing needs. Reservations are not taken, first come, first serve.

Course Highlights:

This nine hole course was constructed by Sam Farris and Son in 1958. It has been a family run facility ever since. It is located just 3 miles north of Sebastopol. It is a short course measuring 1,663 yards. Par is 31 / 33. Four of the holes have a par 4 if you play from the Men's Tees and from the Ladies' Tees, six of the holes are par 4's. There is a water hazard around the green on the 8th hole. Sebastopol annually hosts the Apple Blossom Tournament during the first week in April. There are now new greens on the 1st and 3rd holes. They have also planted trees during the past year.

Sonoma County

164

Copyright 1991 by Locations Plus..

Sonoma Golf Club

17700 Arnold Drive
Boyes Hot Springs, CA 95416

(707) 996-0300

18 Hole Course

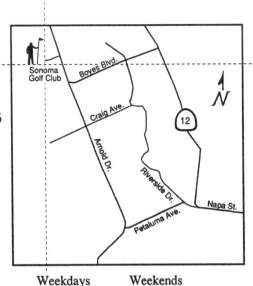

1991 Green Fees:

	Weekdays	Weekends
9 Holes:	n.a.	n.a.
18 Holes:	$60.00	$80.00

Twilight Rates: n.a.
Senior Discount: n.a.

Equipment Rental: Golf Car included in Green Fee

Golf Cars - 9 Holes: Included   Golf Cars - 18 Holes: Included
    Pull Carts: Clubs: $30.00

Amenities:

Club Pro: Ron Blum   Lessons: $30 / 30 Minutes
There is a Practice Putting Green, Chipping Green and Driving
Range available, bucket prices range from $3 to $4.50. Their full
restaurant is open from dawn to dusk. The Pro Shop carries a full
line of merchandise. Reservations can be made up to one week in
advance beginning at day break.

Course Highlights:

Sonoma Golf Club, built in 1926, was formally known as Sonoma
National. The course has just completed a 8 million dollar renova-
tion. All greens have been built to USGA specs, trees were planted,
fairways rebuilt and 2 new lakes were added. A new irrigation
system has been installed to maintain this challenging new course
renovated by Robert Muir Graves. The course plays for a long
7,069 yards from the back tees.

Sonoma
County

Tayman Park Golf Course

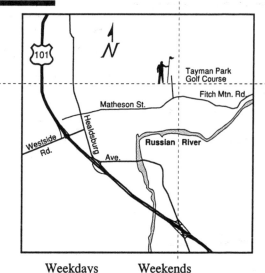

927 S. Fitch Mountain Rd.
Healdsburg, CA 95448

(707) 433-4275

9 Hole Course

1991 Green Fees:

	Weekdays	Weekends
9 Holes:	$8.00	$10.00
18 Holes:	$10.00	$12.00

Twilight Rates: n.a.
Senior Discount: Weekdays only

Equipment Rental:

Golf Cars - 9 Holes: $9.00	Golf Cars - 18 Holes: $16.00
Pull Carts: $2.00	Clubs: $5.00

Amenities:

Club Pro: Mike Ash   Lessons: $20 / Lesson
A Practice Putting Green is available at Tayman Park, but no
Chipping Green or Driving Range. The Tayman Park Bar and Grill
is open from 6 a.m. until 8 p.m. for your convenience. The Pro Shop
handles golfing accessories to help in filling your immediate needs.
Reservations can be made two weeks in advance.

Course Highlights:

This public nine hole course gives you a choice of tees on some of
the holes when playing a full eighteen. The length of the course is
5,349 yards long from the Men's Tees and is rated 64.8. From the
Women's Tees it is 4,952 yards long and is rated 68.4 Overall par is
70. Only one of the holes is a par 5; there are two par 3's and the rest
are par 4's. Except for one fairly severe dogleg, most of the holes are
a straight shot to the green. You have to shoot directly over water on
two of the holes.

Wikiup Golf Course

5001 Carriage Lane
Santa Rosa, CA 95403

(707) 546-8787

9 Hole Course

1991 Green Fees:

	Weekdays	Weekends
9 Holes:	$6.00	$7.00
18 Holes:	$8.00	$9.00

Twilight Rates: n.a.
Senior Discount: Weekdays, $6.00 for 18 holes

Equipment Rental:

Golf Cars - 9 Holes: $9.00	Golf Cars - 18 Holes: $12.00
Pull Carts: $2.00	Clubs: $3.00

Amenities:

Club Pro: n.a.   Lessons: n.a.
A Practice Putting Green is available at Wikiup Golf Course, but no Chipping Green or Driving Range. The Snack Shop is open from 7 a.m. until 6 p.m. serving tasty sandwiches and assorted beverages, including beer and wine. The Pro Shop carries a limited assortment of golf accessories. Reservations are not taken, first come, first serve.

Course Highlights:

This nine hole public course opened in 1963. It has changed hands three times, presently it is being well maintained. There is a little lake sitting across the fairway on the 2nd hole, it also presents a lateral water hazard on holes #5, 6, 7, and 8. It is a pleasant course to play with fairly nice size greens. Total yardage, if playing eighteen holes, is 3,254. It is rated 54.0. Men's par is 58, Women's par is 60. All the holes are par 3's except for #2, and #8. The 8th is a par 5 for the Ladies.

167

Windsor Golf Club

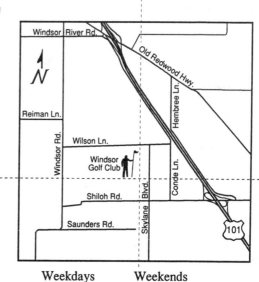

6555 Skylane Boulevard
Windsor, CA 95492

(707) 838-7888

18 Hole Course

1991 Green Fees:

	Weekdays	Weekends
9 Holes:	n.a.	n.a.
18 Holes:	$19.00	$29.00
Twilight Rates:	$13.00	$19.00

Senior Discount: $11.00 Mon., Tues. and Wed.

Equipment Rental:

Golf Cars - 9 Holes:	Golf Cars - 18 Holes: $20.00
Pull Carts: $2.00	Clubs: $10.00

Amenities:

Club Pro: Charlie Gibson   Lessons: $18 / 30 Minutes
Windsor Golf Club offers a Practice Putting Green and a Driving
Range. Bucket prices range from $1 to $3. Their Snack Bar is open
from 7 a.m. until 7 p.m., daily. Their Pro Shop will be able to fill
most of your golfing needs. Reservations can be made seven days in
advance. Their least busy day is Tuesday.

Course Highlights:

This 18 hole championship course sits on 120 acres of rolling
countryside. There is plenty of room between fairways, enough for 5
lakes, a small stream and a couple of marshes. The greens are small
and with all of natures enhancements, this course offers a challenge.
It measures a long 6,650 yards from the Championship Tees and has
a rating of 72.3. From the Blue Tees: 6,169 yds. rated 70.1 / 121,
Regular Tees: 5,628 yds. rated 67.0 / 118, Forward Tees: 5,116 yds.
rated 69.3 / 125. Par for the course is 72. This course hosts the Ben
Hogan Tournament, the Santa Rosa Open and the Hot Air Balloon
Classic.

INDEX BY NAME

INDEX BY NAME

INDEX BY NAME

9 HOLE COURSES

Aetna Springs Golf Course	(707) 965-2115	p. 61
Aptos Par 3	(408) 688-5000	p.136
Bay Meadows Golf Course	(415) 341-7204	p.105
Blackberry Farm Golf Course	(408) 253-9200	p.114
Bolado Park Golf Course	(408) 628-9995	p .86
Buchanan Field Golf Course	(415) 682-1846	p. 27
Campus Commons Golf Course	(916) 922-5861	p. 72
Casserly Par 3 Golf Course	(408) 724-1654	p.139
Chimney Rock Golf Course	(707) 255-3363	p. 63
Cypress Golf Course	(415) 992-5155	p.107
Diablo Hills Golf Course	(415) 939-7372	p. 30
Emerald Hills Golf Club	(415) 368-7820	p.108
Escalon Golf Course	(209) 838-1277	p. 98
Fairgrounds Golf Course	(707) 546-2469	p.155
Fleming Golf Course	(415) 661-1865	p. 91
Foothill Golf Center	(916) 725-3355	p. 79
Gavilan Golf Course	(408) 848-1363	p.117
Gleneagles International Golf Course	(415) 587-2425	p. 92
Golden Gate Park Course	(415) 751-8987	p. 93
Green Tree Golf Course	(707) 448-1420	p.147
King City Golf Course	(408) 385-4546	p. 47
Los Arroyos Golf Course	(707) 938-2868	p.157
Marina Golf Course	(415) 895-2164	p. 15
Mill Valley Golf Course	(415) 388-9982	p. 41
Mount St. Helena Golf Course	(707) 942-9966	p. 65
Northwood Golf Course	(707) 865-1116	p.160
Parkway Golf Course	(415) 565-6862	p. 16
Pine Meadows Public Course	(415) 228-2881	p. 33
Pittsburg Golf & Country Club	(415) 427-4940	p. 34
Pleasanton Fairways Golf Course	(415) 462-4653	p. 17
Pruneridge Golf Club	(408) 248-4424	p.122
Roseville Rolling Greens Golf Course	(916) 797-9986	p. 81
Sea Ranch Golf Links	(707) 785-2467	p.163
Sebastopol Golf Course	(707) 823-9852	p.164
Sherwood Greens Golf Course	(408) 758-7333	p. 56
Springtown Municipal Golf Course	(415) 455-5695	p. 19
Sunken Gardens Municipal Golf Course	(408) 739-6588	p.130
Tayman Park Golf Course	(707) 433-4275	p.166
Valley Gardens Golf Course	(408) 438-3058	p.143
Wikiup Golf Course	(707) 546-8787	p.167
William Land Park Golf Course	(916) 455-5014	p. 82

18 HOLE COURSES

18 HOLE COURSES

Manteca Park Golf Course	(209) 823-5945	p.101
Mountain Shadows Resort Golf Course	(707) 584-7766	p.158-159
Napa Municipal Golf Course	(707) 255-4333	p. 66
Oakmont Golf Course East	(707) 538-2454	p.161
Oakmont Golf Course West	(707) 539-0415	p.162
Pacific Grove Municipal Golf Course	(408) 648-3177	p. 49
Pajaro Valley Golf Club	(408) 724-3851	p. 50
Palo Alto Municipal Golf Course	(415) 856-0881	p.120
Pasatiempo Golf Club	(408) 426-3622	p.141
Peacock Gap Golf & Country Club	(415) 453-4940	p. 42
Pebble Beach Golf Links	(408) 624-6611	p. 51
Pleasant Hills Golf & Country Club	(408) 238-3485	p.121
Poppy Hills Golf Course	(408) 625-2035	p. 52
Rancho Canada Golf Club	(408) 624-0111	p.53-54
Rancho Solano	(707) 429-4653	p.149
Ridgemark Golf & Country Club	(408) 637-1010	p.87-88
Riverside Golf Course	(408) 463-0622	p.123
Salinas Fairway Golf Course	(408) 758-7300	p. 55
San Geronimo Golf Course	(415) 488-4030	p. 43
San Jose Municipal Golf Course	(408) 441-4653	p.124
San Mateo Municipal Golf Course	(415) 347-1461	p.110
San Ramon Royal Vista Golf Club	(415) 828-6100	p. 35
Santa Clara Golf & Tennis Club	(408) 980-9515	p.125
Santa Teresa Golf Club	(408) 225-2650	p.126
Sharp Park Golf Course	(415) 359-3380	p.111
Shoreline Golf Links	(415) 969-2041	p.127
Skywest Golf Course	(415) 278-6188	p. 18
Sonoma Golf Club	(707) 966-0300	p.165
Spring Hills Golf Course	(408) 724-1404	p.142
Spring Valley Golf Course	(408) 262-1722	p.128
Spyglass Hill Golf Course	(408) 624-6611	p. 57
Summit Pointe Golf Club	(408) 262-8813	p.129
Sunnyvale Municipal Golf Course	(408) 738-3666	p.131
Sunol Valley Golf Course	(415) 862-2404	p. 20
Swenson Park Golf Course	(209) 477-0774	p.102
The Island Club Golf Course	(415) 684-2654	p. 36
The Links at Spanish Bay	(408) 624-6611	p. 58
Thunderbird Golf & Country Club	(408) 259-3355	p.132
Tilden Park Golf Course	(415) 848-7373	p. 37
Tony Lema Golf Course	(415) 895-2162	p. 21
Van Buskirk Park Golf Course	(209) 464-5629	p.103
Willow Park Golf Course	(415) 537-8989	p. 22
Windsor Golf Club	(707) 838-7888	p.168

PRIVATE COURSES

Alameda County

Castlewood Country Club	Pleasanton	(415) 846-5151
Claremont Country Club	Oakland	(415) 655-2431
Sequoyah Country Club	Oakland	(415) 632-4069

Contra Costa County

Blackhawk Country Club	Danville	(415) 820-1118
Contra Costa Country Club	Pleasant Hill	(415) 685-8288
Crow Canyon Country Club	Danville	(415) 866-8300
Diablo Country Club	Diablo	(415) 837-9233
Discovery Bay Country Club	Discovery Bay	(415) 634-0700
Mira Vista Country Club	El Cerrito	(415) 237-7045
Moraga Country Club	Moraga	(415) 376-2253
Orinda Country Club	Orinda	(415) 254-0811
Richmond Country Club	Richmond	(415) 232-7815
Rossmoor Golf Course	Walnut Creek	(415) 933-2607
Round Hill Golf & Country Club	Alamo	(415) 837-7424

Marin County

Marin Country Club	Novato	(415) 479-0252
Meadow Country Club	Fairfax	(415) 456-9393

Monterey County

Carmel Valley Golf & Country Club	Carmel Valley	(408) 624-2779
Carmel Valley Ranch	Carmel	(408) 626-2511
Corral de Tierra Country Club	Salinas	(408) 484-1325
Cypress Point Club	Pebble Beach	(408) 624-2223
Fort Ord Golf Course	Fort Ord	(408) 899-0636
Monterey Peninsula Country Club	Pebble Beach	(408) 372-8141
Salinas Golf & Country Club	Salinas	(408) 449-1526
U.S. Navy Golf Course	Monterey	(408) 646-2167

PRIVATE COURSES

Napa County

Meadowood Resort Hotel	St. Helena	(707) 963-3646
Napa Valley Country Club	Napa	(707) 252-1114
Silverado Country Club	Napa	(707) 257-5460

Sacramento County

Del Paso Country Club	Sacramento	(916) 489-3681
Lawrence Links Golf Course	Sacramento	(916) 643-3313
Mather AFB Golf Course	Sacramento	(916) 364-3731
North Ridge Country Club	Fair Oaks	(916) 967-5716
Rancho Murieta County Club	Rancho Murieta	(916) 985-7200
Sunrise Golf Course	Citrus Heights	(916) 723-8854
Valley Hi Country Club	Elk Grove	(916) 423-2170

San Francisco County

Olympic Country Club	San Francisco	(415) 587-8338
Presidio Army Golf Course	Presidio	(415) 751-1322
San Francisco Golf Club	San Francisco	(415) 469-4122

San Joaquin County

Elkhorn Country Club	Stockton	(209) 477-0252
Spring Creek Golf & Country Club	Ripon	(209) 599-3630
Stockton Golf & Country Club	Stockton	(209) 466-6221
Tracy Golf & Country Club	Stockton	(209) 835-9463
Woodbridge Golf & Country Club	Woodbridge	(209) 369-2371

PRIVATE COURSES

San Mateo County

Burlingame Country Club	Hillsborough	(415) 342-0750
California Golf Club	S. San Francisco	(415) 589-0144
Green Hills Country Club	Milbrae	(415) 583-0882
Lake Merced Golf & Country Club	Daly City	(415) 755-2239
Menlo Country Club	Woodside	(415) 366-9910
Moffett Field Golf Course	NAS Moffett Field	(415) 966-5332
Peninsula Golf & Country Club	San Mateo	(415) 345-9521
Sharon Heights Golf & Country Club	Menlo Park	(415) 854-6429

Santa Clara County

Almaden Golf & Country Club	San Jose	(408) 268-4653
La Rinconada Country Club	Los Gatos	(408) 395-4220
Los Altos Golf & Country Club	Los Altos	(415) 948-2146
Palo Alto Hills Country Club	Palto Alto	(415) 948-2320
San Jose Country Club	San Jose	(408) 258-3636
Saratoga Country Club	Saratoga	(408) 253-5494
Stanford Golf Course	Stanford	(415) 323-0944
The Villages Golf & Country Club	San Jose	(408) 274-3220

Solano County

Green Valley Country Club	Suisun City	(707) 864-0473

Sonoma County

Petaluma Golf & Country Club	Petaluma	(707) 762-7041
Santa Rosa Golf & Country Club	Santa Rosa	(707) 564-6617

GOLF BUDDIES PHONE LIST

Name	Address	Phone

**TEE TIMES
CALENDAR
1991-1992**

April 1991 - Tee Times

SUN	MON	TUES	WED	THUR	FRI	SAT
	1	2	3	4	5	6
7	8	9	10	11	12	13
14	15	16	17	18	19	20
21	22	23	24	25	26	27
28	29	30				

Golf Notes and Other Important Facts

_____

_____

_____

_____

_____

May 1991 - Tee Times

SUN	MON	TUES	WED	THUR	FRI	SAT
			1	2	3	4
5 Mother's Day	6	7	8	9	10	11
12	13	14	15	16	17	18
19	20	21	22	23	24	25
26	27 Memorial Day	28	29	30	31	

Golf Notes and Other Important Facts

_____

_____

_____

_____

_____

June 1991 - Tee Times

SUN	MON	TUES	WED	THUR	FRI	SAT
						1
2	3	4	5	6	7	8
9	10	11	12	13	14	15
Father's Day 16	17	18	19	20	21	22
23/30	24	25	26	27	28	29

Golf Notes and Other Important Facts

_____

_____

_____

_____

_____

_____

July 1991 - Tee Times

SUN	MON	TUES	WED	THUR Independence Day	FRI	SAT
	1	2	3	4	5	6
7	8	9	10	11	12	13
14	15	16	17	18	19	20
21	22	23	24	25	26	27
28	29	30	31			

Golf Notes and Other Important Facts

_____

_____

_____

_____

_____

August 1991 - Tee Times

SUN	MON	TUES	WED	THUR	FRI	SAT
				1	2	3
4	5	6	7	8	9	10
11	12	13	14	15	16	17
18	19	20	21	22	23	24
25	26	27	28	29	30	31

Golf Notes and Other Important Facts

September 1991 - Tee Times

SUN	MON	TUES	WED	THUR	FRI	SAT
1	Labor Day 2	3	4	5	6	7
8	9	10	11	12	13	14
15	16	17	Yom Kippur 18	19	20	21
22	23	24	25	26	27	28
29	30					

Golf Notes and Other Important Facts

_____

_____

_____

_____

_____

October 1991 - Tee Times

SUN	MON	TUES	WED	THUR	FRI	SAT
		1	2	3	4	5
6	7 Columbus Day	8	9	10	11	12
13	14	15	16	17	18	19
20	21	22	23	24	25	26
27	28	29	30	31 Halloween		

Golf Notes and Other Important Facts

_____

_____

_____

_____

_____

November 1991 - Tee Times

SUN	MON	TUES	WED	THUR	FRI	SAT
					1	2
10	Veterans' Day 11	12	13	14	15	16
17	18	19	20	21	22	23
24	25	26	27	Thanksgiving Day 28	29	30

Golf Notes and Other Important Facts

_____

_____

_____

_____

_____

_____

December 1991 - Tee Times

SUN	MON Hanukkah	TUES	WED	THUR	FRI	SAT
1	2	3	4	5	6	7
8	9	10	11	12	13	14
15	16	17	18	19	20	21
22	23	24	25 Christmas Day	26	27	28
29	30	31				

Golf Notes and Other Important Facts

_____

_____

_____

_____

_____

January 1992- Tee Times

SUN	MON	TUES	WED New Year's Day 1	THUR 2	FRI 3	SAT 4
5	6	7	8	9	10	11
12	13	14	15	16	17	18
19	20	21	22	23	24	25
26	27	28	29	30	31	

Golf Notes and Other Important Facts

_____

_____

_____

_____

_____

_____

February 1992 - Tee Times

SUN	MON	TUES	WED	THUR	FRI	SAT
						1
2	3	4	5	6	7	8
			Lincoln's Birthday		Valentine's Day	
9	10	11	12	13	14	15
						Washington's Birthday
16	17	18	19	20	21	22
23	24	25	26	27	28	29

Golf Notes and Other Important Facts

_____

_____

_____

_____

_____

_____

March 1992 - Tee Times

SUN	MON	TUES	WED	THUR	FRI	SAT
1	2	3	4	5	6	7
8	9	10	11	12	13	14
15	16	17	18	19	20	21
22	23	24	25	26	27	28
29	30	31				

Golf Notes and Other Important Facts

_____

_____

_____

_____

_____

_____

Locations Plus... for L.A.

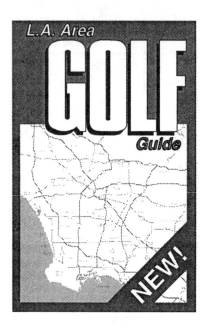